19: PERSPECTIVES IN CRITICISM

PERSPECTIVES IN CRITICISM

19:

FRANK LENTRICCHIA

The Gaiety of Language:
An Essay on the Radical Poetics of W. B. Yeats and Wallace Stevens

UNIVERSITY OF CALIFORNIA PRESS
Berkeley and Los Angeles
1968

68-9239

University of California Press
Berkeley and Los Angeles, California
Cambridge University Press
London, England

LIBRARY OF CONGRESS CATALOG CARD NO. 68-14019
Printed in the United States of America

To my mother and father,
i migliori parenti

Natives of poverty, children of malheur,
The gaiety of language is our seigneur.

WALLACE STEVENS,
"Esthetique du Mal"

Follow, poet, follow right
To the bottom of the night,
With your unconstraining voice
Still persuade us to rejoice;

With the farming of a verse
Make a vineyard of the curse,
Sing of human unsuccess
In a rapture of distress;

In the deserts of the heart
Let the healing fountain start,
In the prison of his days
Teach the free man how to praise.

W. H. AUDEN,
"In Memory of W. B. Yeats"

Preface

WHILE PLANNING AND WRITING this essay during the past two and a half years I have been given the help, and encouragement, too, of more people than I can remember or than I have space to acknowledge. I would like to thank my friends at Duke University—William Arfin, John Cunningham, Frank Gado, Philip Mancha, Richard Neubauer, and Eric Taylor—for their assistance, and Conrad Sugar who always gave freely of his time and energy. Professor Grover Smith, also of Duke, sparked my studies of Yeats in a graduate seminar. At the University of California, Los Angeles, Robert Maniquis and Blake Nevius did more than they had to do, reading the manuscript and listening to my complaints and questions, minor and major.

Murray Krieger and Hazard Adams of the University of California, Irvine, read the manuscript, made many helpful suggestions, and expressed the kind of interest and faith in my work which makes one feel lucky to be in the profession. I wish that I could adequately thank my hometown friend, Eugene Nassar, author of a superb book on Stevens, who taught me much more about literature and criticism than he will ever realize. Bernard Duffey of Duke was the shaping spirit of my work. He introduced me to literary theory, directed an earlier version of this essay as a doctoral dissertation, and influenced me in ways too subtle to identify and too obvious to mention.

I would like to thank Herbert Schueller of the *Journal of Aesthetics and Art Criticism* for allowing me to reprint, in somewhat altered form, "Four Types of Nineteenth-Century Poetic" (chapter 1). "Wallace Stevens: The Ironic Eye" (a portion of chapter 6) is reprinted in altered form from *The Yale Review,* copyright Yale University.

My wife Karen made the final revisions a pleasure to do. Last, for the people to whom this book is dedicated, it is impossible to summon the proper words of gratitude and admiration.

F. L.

Contents

1

Introduction

THIS STUDY is intended as an essay in definition, and my
first aim is relatively circumscribed: to explain the
poetics of William Butler Yeats and Wallace Stevens.
From the moment I began planning the essay, however, I was convinced that a detailed analysis of the
prose work of Yeats and Stevens would be most meaningful if placed in the broad spectrum of postromantic
literary theory. And here is where the problems begin.
Should one choose, for example, the perspective of
modern "contextual" theory, the theory of the self-
sufficiency of the poetic symbol, or should one assume
(as many do) that self-sufficiency theories are really
the New Critics' restatements of Coleridgean poetic,
and not "new" at all? The latter alternative leads to the
popular "romantic" interpretation of modern poetry,
the former to the familiar remarks about modern poetry's radical break with the past (with the exception, of
course, of a certain group of seventeenth-century poets). I take the position below that neither alternative
is adequate, that, in general, Yeats and Stevens do not
fit the critical concepts of the nineteenth century
which I try to redefine on a comparative basis in chapter 2.

The question of the relationship between modern
poetry and romantic literary theory has been hotly argued; until the past few years the answers tended to

1

cancel each other. For example, according to T. E. Hulme, T. S. Eliot, I. A. Richards, and the New Critics in general, ours is an antiromantic literature and criticism. Yet, for Edmund Wilson, Jacques Barzun, Frank Kermode, and Richard Foster, among a legion of others, the twentieth century is a romantic era in disguise.[1] It seems that in the 1960's the romanticist views are prevailing; judging by the pervasive influence of the "visionary" (or mythic) school of criticism, antiromanticism is not only passé, but naïve besides. The brilliant master of the visionaries is clearly Northrop Frye; and though he may be less than happy about being made the unerring authority, a good many of his disciples—notably Harold Bloom[2]—have asked us to read modern poets (especially Yeats and Stevens) as variations on, and even culminations of, the apocalyptic mood of William Blake. The visionaries have not been sympathetic toward the New Criticism's contextual theory because their main interest is in *classification* by way of myth and archetype, whereas the contextual critic is most interested in the *specification* of a work's uniqueness. Sometimes they have not been generous either, for contextualism, they tell us, is merely a sterilizing formalization of romantic organicism.

The greatest harassment to the student of modern poetics and poetry would appear to be, then, his own critical categories and allegiances. Far too often, he learns, critical categories beg, rather than answer, his questions; far too often he finds the categories themselves becoming the spectacles through which he sees, and therefore understands, a Yeats or a Stevens. This essay attempts to remove the spectacles we have inherited from the nineteenth century.

In chapter 2 I outline and treat comparatively four types of nineteenth-century poetic, while trying to render with some precision the various views of reality and epistemology which function as a matrix for these literary theories. The focus for the discussion is the

2

antithetical aesthetic ideas of Immanuel Kant and F. W. J. Schelling. In Kant's *Critique of Aesthetic Judgment* I find the germinal suggestion of an autonomous artistic imagination that is grounded in and limited by the very medium in which it chooses to express itself. Contrarily, Schelling's *System of Transcendental Idealism* presents an artistic imagination so powerful and so encompassing that it consumes both the ethical and the cognitive as it flies beyond its medium and penetrates to a deeper ontological structure of the natural world. I suggest (1) that Kant and Schelling can be seen as the guiding symbolic forces of the major nineteenth-century literary theories; (2) that Coleridge, as chief English romantic idealist,* falls mainly within Schelling's scheme; (3) that Zola, in his naturalism, denies utterly the transcendental extension of the material world while holding onto a view of poetic value which parallels the romantic view; and (4) that the symbolists give us two opposing but, I think, new approaches.

Both approaches of symbolism are anchored in

* Here and throughout the book I have considered Coleridge from the perspective of Schellingian transcendentalism. I am well aware that the transcendental idealist is not the whole Coleridge, but I am prepared to argue that the transcendental idealist is the essential Coleridge. Even in such a piece as "On the Principles of Genial Criticism," where there is a heavy Kantian influence—where, that is, there is an attempt to distinguish the aesthetic realm as unique—the presence of a universalizing, Platonic interest is unmistakable when Coleridge quotes, toward the essay's conclusion, a passage from Plotinus as an explication for "Dejection: An Ode." In that same essay there is an insistence upon the "pre-established harmony between nature and the human mind." It is this harmony, grounded in the Schellingian Absolute, which enables the imagination to reconcile opposites, to overcome (in epistemological terms) the subject-object division. The finite particulars of nature are cherished, it seems to me, because they look out on the Absolute. But, it is true, Coleridge is complicated beyond what most of us can credit him for. Even as he speaks of the reconciliation of opposites, a phrase suggesting his thoroughly idealistic obsession with unity, he speaks of the balance of the discordant, a phrase suggestive of an idea sympathetic to the contextualist's obsessions with paradox, with tension, with unresolved conflict.

3

Zola's materialistic universe; both attempt to establish a theory of poetic value centered on the idea that poems have unique reasons for being. Whereas one symbolist approach assigns the artist powers of magic and the occult, the other gives him a constructive imagination that can create in language a verbal universe complete and sufficient unto itself. The magical symbolist rests his view of poetry not so much on his ability to do something with language which no one else can do, but on the idea that the imagination can spring him out of a naturalistic reality and give him special access to a realm of Beauty which he then allows us to perceive *through* his poems. Unlike the romantic idealist, the symbolist looks upon nature as the alien, matter wholly matter, and not as the continuum of self and spirit. The symbolist imagination must either leap over nature (magical symbolism) or ignore it by creating its own "nature" in language (constructive symbolism). (The magical imagination seems to have been primarily a phenomenon of later nineteenth-century France; the constructive imagination, implicit in Kant, has been developed into the aesthetic of modern contextualism.)

I realize that a comprehensive treatment of any one of the people I discuss in chapter 2 could easily run to a volume in length. Let me say now that I am not interested in exploring the complexities of any given figure, but only in using that figure as a vehicle to present an idea about the nature of poetry. For example, with Coleridge I am interested solely in his romantic idealism as it grows out of Schelling and as it bears on his conception of poetic value. As I see it, therefore, the role of chapter 2 is like that of a theoretical lexicon. And that, in fact, is the way I have used it. In chapters 3 and 5, I offer readings of the explicit poetics of Yeats and Stevens by probing for their answers to essentially three questions: How do they define the reality within which the imagination must operate? What are the

4

powers and limits of the imagination? What do they understand to be the nature and value of a poem? Whenever possible, I contrast their views on poetry with the views they inherited from the nineteenth century. For easy reference, and for the sake of comparison, I have placed capsule summaries of the romantic, naturalist, and symbolist theories of poetry before the appropriate subdivisions in chapter 2. Throughout the essay I use as a focal point a rather ideal formulation of the contextual poetic in the hope of gaining perspective on all theories that I consider.

Chapters 4 and 6 are studies of the implicitly theoretical poems of Yeats and Stevens. These poems about poetry immediately confront us with a bothersome question: Are they "doctrinal" poems in the sense that they can be reduced to a proposition about the theory of poetry, and hence, some would say, not poems at all but watered-down philosophy? Or do the doctrines simply provide the donnée, the matter that is then transformed into a verbal entity which balks at propositional reduction? If the poems are simply decorated doctrine then we may use them, or "mine" them, for theoretical statement. We may quote a passage and say with confidence that *this* is what Stevens thinks about the imagination. The view offered below is that these poems about poetry are not sugarcoated pills of doctrine. In them I see not merely one doctrine presented, but a host of doctrines, some of which imply mutually exclusive ideas about poetry's role and value. Within the context of a single rich poem or passage we see Yeats and Stevens articulating their highest hopes and worst fears, writing as men of feeling, as well as men of thought, of their ambiguous and often flatly contradictory postures toward the poetic imagination. My purpose in chapters 3 and 5 is to illuminate a theoretical position; in chapters 4 and 6 my purpose is critical insofar as I hope to define the complex and deeply mixed tone of their poems. Ultimately, the

5

point I would make about the poems of Yeats and Stevens is that they are not to be looked upon simply as
statements about the theory of poetry to which they
assent. Usually, they saved pure doctrinal meditation
for prose. In a very real sense, their poems speak about
the poverty and the limits of their own theories of
poetry, and in so speaking generate a longing, a desire,
for all those views to which they cannot honestly commit themselves in prose. It is to the poems, then, that
we must look if we wish to see the whole Stevens, the
whole Yeats.

I have had serious misgivings about offering the
phrase "poetics of will" as a description of the theories
of Yeats and Stevens. The word "will" calls up meanings
I do not wish at all to imply.* This is a brief statement
of the idea I have in mind: by conceiving of imagina-

* My "poetics of will" is actually a "poetics of anti-will," if the
nineteenth-century meaning of "will" is insisted upon. I refer the
reader to Murray Krieger's fine article, "The Existential Basis of Contextual Criticism," now reprinted in his *The Play and Place of Criticism* (Baltimore, 1967). Anti-will, as Krieger shows, is the aesthetic
imagination seen in the Kantian and neo-Kantian perspective of dis-
interest, of love for the particulars of nature as particulars, as utterly
unique phenomena which do not yield to the particular-consuming
universal. The poetic imagination as anti-will attends to language
in the same way that it attends to the particulars of the world's body:
with a love for words as words, for artifice as artifice. Such cherishing
of language frees language from its propositional and purely referential task of classification, of devouring the particulars for the sake of
the universal, for the sake of giving us viable modes of communication and action in the everyday world. Only in imaginative contemplation do we truly see the world as it is; only in the successfully
wrought poem do words function in such a way as to capture the
thing as thing without utility value: an object become subject, in
Krieger's terms. An aesthetic object so conceived—as a closed system
of unique and discrete particulars—has certain thematic-moral implications which do not concern me here. I would suggest Krieger's
The Tragic Vision for those who would like to follow the problem.
Yeats and Stevens see the imagination playing with language much
as Krieger's contextualist-existentialist poet plays with language, but
without the (for Krieger) correlative thematic implications. I find it
reassuring that Krieger asserts, without reservation, that *his* Coleridge
(the embryo contextualist-existentialist) is not the dominant Coleridge, but the subordinate to the transcendental idealist.

tion as will, as a purely finite instrument for the channeling and releasing of artistic energy; by pressing for imagination's complete freedom from the Freudian self and the Sartrean "absurd" universe; and, finally, by allowing imagination to play in the linguistic medium without preordained interests, metaphysical, empirical, or communicative—in these ways Yeats and Stevens give back to the poem, on its own irreducible terms, a necessary and valuable role in culture. It is no longer, sad to say, the role that Coleridge and Mallarmé envisioned. The modern imagination is impoverished in comparison, for neither it nor the context within which it functions is so alive with transcendental significance. Poems may only be poems now, not a special way to truth, not a metaphysical apprehension of reality. Simply by being such, however, they play an indispensable role in our lives: for the poet who makes them they allow him, in the very process of making, a moment of freedom and victory over that turmoil of the inner self which always demands expression and which he must suppress, and a release from (though hardly a denial of) the reality of twentieth-century life which shouts down his efforts as little, insipid, and unimportant. We who do not possess such creative genius are given the opportunity to read well and so make the poet's imagination, however briefly, ours. Stevens liked to say that poetry contributes to our happiness, that it helps us to live our lives. We need not ask for more.

2

Four Types of Nineteenth-Century Poetic

ROMANTIC THEORY: THE IDEALISTIC IMAGINATION

THE CORE IDEA of romantic theory in England, in America, and on the Continent as well is the belief that self and nature, imagination and reality—epistemologically, subject and object—stand in interdependent and coherent relation.[1] This postulate is rooted, ultimately, in the assumption of Schelling's idealistic metaphysics (in contrast with Kant's aesthetics) that the finite self and nature exist in a preestablished harmony that is grounded in the "Absolute," or transcendent, spiritual structure of reality. The romantic imagination, then, has access to the idealistic universe because it is continuous with spirit: and spirit is no less than the fact of coalescence and identity of the aesthetic, the cognitive, and the ethical realms.

Coleridge

At one time the claim of the New Critics that a poem is a "contextual," or a self-contained and self-sufficient, thing was enough to start a small academic war. Now, many books later, such critical terms as *autonomous* (self-governing), *autotelic* (having its own end or pur-

8

pose), and *heterocosmic* (a unique world) have become standard weapons in the critical arsenal.[2] Equally standard these days, perhaps even a cliché, is the easy generalization that contextualism is simply a disguised romanticism, and that Coleridge either said it or implied it all before. Probably the most influential and direct statements of this idea are in Frank Kermode's *Romantic Image* and Richard Foster's *The New Romantics*.

I agree with M. H. Abrams' assessment of Kermode: "Modern theory has parallels with single concepts in the English Romantic writers, but it is a fallacy to identify the product with the origins. Taken in their totality, in fact, the major Romantic theories of poetry are at the opposite pole from contemporary notions of the . . . autonomous image."[3] I wish now to explore Coleridge's tendency toward Schelling's romantic idealism, and the opposite tendency of modern contextualists (and nineteenth-century symbolists) toward Kant's concept of the autotelic existence of the work of art. Such an exploration will show that Coleridge's idea of the imagination, when placed in the framework of his idealistic philosophy, does not postulate the self-sufficiency of the poetic context; nor, in fact, would it find self-sufficiency desirable. In order to separate even more clearly the concepts of "romantic," "symbolist," and "contextualist," I offer some remarks too on the naturalistic bias of symbolist and contextualist theory.

A minimal answer to the question of Coleridge's debt to Kant would necessarily include the notion of mind as the ordering center of perception. In Kant's *Critique of Pure Reason*—one of the sources of Coleridge's view of mind—the faculty called *Verstand* (Understanding) was made constitutive of the phenomenal world. Understanding was defined by Kant as the a priori source of the "forms" of knowledge, whereas the "matter" of knowledge, he believed, was always

9

given in experience and through the senses. The act of knowing, then, was composed of an a priori "form" imposed upon experientially given "content." [4] In opposition to the passive view of Lockean empiricism, Kant saw mind as an active force that molded our conceptions of reality. But it can hardly be overstressed, as we contrast Coleridge and Kant, that Understanding was strictly a scientific faculty, a way of formulating the phenomenal world. Only in a very general sense does Kant's scientific faculty resemble Wordsworth's or Coleridge's poetic imagination, and never does it penetrate phenomenal nature to a world of essence. Actually, Kant emphasized that Understanding could know neither nature in itself nor the noumenal (or spiritual) world because one could never get outside his a priori categories: or, more technically, noumenal reality has no "schema." [5]

Coleridge appropriated the broad idea of Kantian epistemology outlined above. Like Wordsworth's light of the mind which bestowed new splendor on the world of things, the Coleridgean imagination made the raw material of experience meaningful by placing it in unique perspective. For Coleridge, the poet was a metaphorical Kantian, bathing and conditioning for us the external world with subjectively derived aesthetic quality: "Who has not a thousand times seen snow fall on water? Who has not watched it with a new feeling from the time he has read Burns' comparison?" [6] In a now-famous metaphor he put it this way: "The razor's edge becomes a saw to the armed vision." [7] And here, finally, Coleridge would appear to be stating the Kantian theory that lay in the background of his view of the imagination: "We learn all things indeed by occasion of experience; but the very facts so learnt force us inward on the antecedents, that must be presupposed in order to render experience itself possible." [8]

Coleridge's interest in Kant's epistemology seems not to go very far beyond this notion of mind as an active, molding force.* As we read further in the *Biographia Literaria* we find him discarding Kant and picking up Schelling, a thinker more sympathetic to his interests. Kant's conservatism with regard to the *Ding an sich* seems to have been the bone in the throat: "In spite of his [Kant's] declaration, I could never believe it was possible for him to have meant no more by his *Noumenon, or Thing in Itself, than his mere words express;* or that in his own conception he confined the whole plastic power [imagination] to the forms of intellect." [9] Though Coleridge could not believe it, this was precisely what Kant did mean. He must have realized it was so because he turned to another German, who was dissatisfied with Kant's idea of *Ding an sich* because he felt that it ultimately divided subject and object: "In Schelling's *Natur-Philosophie,* and the *System des Transcendentalen Idealismus,* I first found a genial coincidence with much that I had toiled out for myself, and a powerful assistance in what I had yet to do." [10] Basically, and very simply, Coleridge's dissatisfaction with Kant and his ensuing excursion into the philosophy of Schelling symbolized his need for an approach to the theory of knowledge which would push him beyond the limits of the phenomenal world, and beyond the limits of finitude. Through Schelling, Coleridge was given access to nature in itself and the spiritual reality active in it. As René Wellek so aptly phrases it, Schelling ignored all Kant's distinctions "between epistemology, ethics, and aesthetics" and saw the artist as the king of philosophers who could penetrate by intuition or imagination "the essence of the universe, the absolute." [11] By rejecting Kant's warnings about the cognitively inaccessible noumenal reality, Schelling could de-

---

* I refer the reader to the two long footnotes in chapter 1. I do not wish to ignore the complexities of Coleridge, but only to emphasize what I take to be his dominant ideas. See René Wellek, *Immanuel Kant in England* (Princeton, 1931), for a full treatment of the German's influence on Coleridge.

fine the highest act of knowledge as a coherence of subject and noumenal reality. He was then free to ascribe powers to the poetic mind not allowed by Kant, and thus establish a context wherein poems functioned as foyers to an idealistic universe.

It is not very difficult to understand why Schelling's *System of Transcendental Idealism* was so appealing to Coleridge. First of all, Schelling met the very question that Coleridge considered in chapter xii of the *Biographia Literaria:* [12] how is knowledge possible? Schelling answered the question by positing a transcendental monism. And by elevating "artistic intuition" to the position of highest cognitive faculty of the mind, Schelling gave the artist himself the ultimate of autonomous sanctions.

Unlike Kant, Schelling insisted that knowledge itself could not be possible unless there was a fusion of subject and object. In Kant's epistemology there was not fusion, but imposition: perceiver and thing perceived faced each other as like and unlike. Not so in Schelling:

> We cannot comprehend how at one and the same time the objective world should adapt itself to representations in us and representations in us to the objective world, unless there exists a pre-established harmony between the two worlds, the ideal world and the real. . . . this pre-established harmony is real. . . .[13]

The "pre-established harmony" is derived, of course, from the *sine qua non* of idealistic metaphysics: the "Absolute." [14] Schelling completes his argument when he gives "artistic intuition" the role of knowing the Absolute, and the work of art the power of "transporting us to an ideal world" by functioning like a foyer through which we walk in order to enter the ideal. A "great painting," as he suggested, "is merely the opening." [15]

Like Schelling, Coleridge proposed the metaphysics

12

of spirit (the Absolute) for the matrix of his theory of knowledge: ". . . spirit is not originally an object, . . . spirit cannot originally be finite. But neither can it be a subject without becoming an object, and as it is originally the identity of both it can be conceived neither as infinite nor finite exclusively, but as the most original union of both." [16] Or, somewhat more emphatically, "the true system of natural philosophy places the sole reality of things in an absolute which is at once *causa sui et effectus* . . . in the absolute identity of subject and object, which it calls nature. . . ." [17] Nature, thus conceived, is not simply external reality, but the interdependence and interpenetration of self and "external" reality. This spiritual continuity of subject and object is the major theme of romantic literary theory.

Coleridge's philosophical speculations immediately precede the chapter in the *Biographia Literaria* in which he offers his famous definitions of imagination. Had his thought not been informed by Schelling's, his grammar of the imagination would have been opaque indeed. With Schelling, however, it becomes clear that Coleridge assumed cognitive access to a transcendental reality. For spirit, subsisting in the natural world, inheres in the perceiving self as well: "All the organs of spirit are framed for a correspondent world of spirit: . . . they exist in all." [18] His sense of the continuity of spirit is most strongly felt in the sixth and seventh theses: if one becomes aware of himself as a self one becomes aware of his essence as a separate spirit. Only then is there a possibility of unity, of a beneficent harmony with a greater self, a greater spirit: ". . . we elevate our conception to the absolute self, the great eternal I Am, . . . the principle of being, . . . of knowledge, of idea, and of reality; the ground of existence, and the ground of the knowledge of existence. . . ." [19] I would suggest that the continuity of self and nature in spirit becomes for Coleridge both the ultimate source and the ultimate end of cognition and poetry because infinite spirit is the continuum itself on which self and nature reciprocally exist and feed. The principal faculty for Coleridge is not therefore Kant's Understanding, which is limited to a scientific knowledge of finite, phenomenal nature, but Schelling's "artistic intuition" which, since it is "identical" with noumenal reality, is capable of knowing noumenal reality. Given the idealistic world view, the act of knowing the infinite through the finite particulars of nature is synonymous with the act of poetic perception.

We come now to Coleridge's rather enigmatic dictum: "The primary Imagination I hold to be the living power and prime agent of all human perception, and as a repetition in the finite mind of the eternal act of creation in the infinite I Am." [20] I take the key words here to be "finite mind." The statement is not a theory of the literally constructive imagination. Only the infinite mind is capable of creation *ex nihilo*. The primary imagination, fully developed only in the finite mind of the artist, constitutes the natural world as spiritually alive and organically whole because it is continuous with the idealistic reality of which is has cognizance. The power and the value of the romantic poet lie precisely in his awareness that he is fused to spirit through nature, and this awareness is no less than the visionary support and meaning of his poems, the transcendent penetration of the primary imagination.

Romantic Poetry as Knowledge: Idealistic Transparency

Rightly viewed no meanest object is insignificant; all objects are as windows, through which the philosophic eye looks into Infinitude itself.

Sartor Resartus, Bk. I, Ch. XI

In modern contextual theory, a poem is seen as a self-existing, self-sufficient system of language whose form

14

and content are reciprocally caused, whose parts as opposed to its whole are impossible to distinguish because the poem does not exist before it becomes articulated in language. If a poem is to exist in this way, then the poetic imagination cannot function interdependently with nature, or more grandly, with reality. To put it positively: if a form-content split is to be avoided, then the imagination must be grounded in language itself.[21] Meaning (or content) will thus not be found in the "objective" world, or in the poet's mind and emotions, or in a confluence of the two as romanticism would have it, but wholly within the peculiar context of language which is simultaneously the poem's form and its meaning. Poetic language, therefore, is neither decoration for an idea, nor (to use Murray Krieger's metaphor [22]) a clear, transparent window through which we are allowed to see the world or the poet's inner life. Language is opaque, the window has been painted black, and the poem resides in language alone. The philosophical source for contextual thinking lies not in Schelling's transcendental monism, which Coleridge found attractive, but in Kant's notion of the autonomy or singularity of the aesthetic realm, which Coleridge did not accept.[23]

I have suggested that a number of critics assume romantic aesthetics to be the source for a theory of contextualism. Such a view is possible, it seems to me, only if one disregards the relevance of idealistic philosophy to the romantic understanding of the creative process. In romantic theory the role of language is simply not exclusively primary in the contextualist sense, and idealistic philosophy—the frame for Coleridge's thought—is a central reason. A romantic poem is useful and romantic poetry in general is "poetry with a purpose," as Abrams has said.[24] Briefly, I would say that the function and the value of a romantic poem are to serve as an opening to the idealistic universe whose structure—spirit, the identity of

15

beauty, truth, and goodness—is apprehended in that coherent intuition of the artist which, in an act of radical reconciliation, dissolves the subject-object division. In romantic theory only the act of perception is organic or self-sufficient, and the poem's ultimate function is to window that act. Thus, poetry yields the highest knowledge because *through* its language we can see the interpenetration of poetic mind and nature which reveals spirit. Art, as Schelling suggests, transports us to the ideal. A romantic idealist must hold that finally a form-content split is desirable: language is form, the transparent entity that windows idealistic content which, by definition, is visionary and not linguistic.

A few concrete instances: Emerson postulated a version of Schelling's monism when he wrote in "The Poet" that there are three children of the universe: the knower (lover of truth), the doer (lover of good), and the sayer or poet (lover of beauty), each having the "powers of the other latent in him." [25] Coleridge thought that the poet would "moralize his readers" and "delight and improve us by [his] sentiments." [26] And, as a monist, he could not make the sharp distinction between science and poetry which a contextualist makes.[27] Perhaps Coleridge's statement about the secondary imagination makes the point best:

> The secondary Imagination I consider as an echo of the former, co-existing with the conscious will, yet still as identical with the primary in the *kind* of its agency, and differing only in *degree,* and in the *mode* of its operation. It dissolves, diffuses, dissipates, in order to recreate: or where this process is rendered impossible, yet still at all events it struggles to idealize and to unify. It is essentially *vital,* even as all objects (*as* objects) are essentially fixed and dead.[28]

The primary imagination as the cognitive faculty is not substantively different from the secondary imagination, the artistic faculty. The cognitive act of coherent intuition belongs essentially to the primary imagination, while the act of aesthetic creativity belongs essentially to the secondary imagination. The secondary imagination may be said to be "creative" insofar as it imparts "life"—its own vitality—to a world of dead objects. But this vitality is derived from (or "echoes," to use Coleridge's word) the organic union of subject and object which is already completed in the primary imagination (the *living* power) at a mental level. In the writing of poetry, the "conscious will" must come into play in an effort to so arrange language (form) that the reader may see through it to that fusion of primary imagination and reality which reveals, in contrast with the world of dead objects (the world of "ordinary" perception), the living vitality of the idealistic universe, the efflux from the Absolute.

The implicit form-content split suggested by Coleridge's two imaginations raises again the issue of the organicism or self-sufficiency of the poem itself. On this point Schelling provides the salient clue to Coleridge's thinking. Coleridge's conception of the secondary imagination implies that it is the source of form—the shaping of language—which imprinted on vision becomes for the reader a window to vision whose source is the primary imagination. This is in line with Schelling's suggestion that the aesthetic object is the "inverse of the organic product of nature" since in the aesthetic object form and content are separable: [29] "form" is achieved through shaping of language, whereas "content" is supplied in vision. Hence, when Coleridge described the essence of a poem with biological metaphors he could not mean that a poem is an utterly self-sustaining entity. It would appear he meant that forms should not be cavalierly imposed on ideas as mere decoration; that poets should not be imitators of Pope; that poems, in short, in opposition to the studied effects of neoclassical artifice, should seem spontaneous and natural. I doubt that Coleridge would sympathize

17

with the notion that a poem is organic in the literal sense. For him, poems must "mean," not "be." And why should not poems "mean" when the meaning is the highest philosophical truth? In a piece heavily indebted to Schelling, Coleridge put it this way: the artist must "imitate"—or, in our terminology, "window" —not "mere nature, the *natura naturata*," but the "*natura naturans*, which presupposes a bond between nature in the higher sense and the soul of man." [30]

Assuming, however, that critics will continue to use the organic metaphor, it may be worthwhile to distinguish two senses of that metaphor: the first, which appears to be Coleridge's sense, postulates an idea about an alogical principle of unification among disparate elements in good poems; the second, a contextual usage, incorporates this idea of Coleridge's but goes far beyond it by postulating absolute coherence of form and content—a theory, in so many words, of the purely immanent nature of poetic meaning. Coleridge's point has been very well taken by practical critics of the twentieth century; the contextual theory, on the other hand, seems to have found a welcome place within the provinces of certain modern aestheticians.

There is a more dramatic way of measuring the distance between Coleridgean organicism and recent contextual organicism. For Coleridge, the organic metaphor has implications for his idealistic metaphysics. He can see the harmonious integration of parts in a poem resolving all tension, thematic as well as aesthetic. The unity and harmony of the poem reflect the unity and harmony of the universe. The poem, then, is a suggestive analogy, a metaphor, for the metaphysically organic harmony of nature. In the essay "On Poesy or Art," Coleridge sees the poem—insofar as it is like an organism, a "unity in multeity"—as window to the Schellingian universe which, in ordinary perception, is a world of dead objects, a "multeity" without

18

"unity." Schelling himself put it this way in "On the Relations of the Plastic Arts to Nature," an essay Coleridge undoubtedly studied for his own "On Poesy or Art": ". . . to one, Nature is nothing more than the lifeless aggregate of an interminable crowd of objects, or the space in which, as in a vessel, he imagines things placed . . . to the inspired seeker alone, the holy, ever-creative original energy of the world, which generates and . . . evolves all things out of itself."

Now, in opposition to Coleridge, who believes, in the conclusion of "On Poesy or Art," that "strife" and the "manifold" are overcome in beauty, the contextual theorist must never, as Krieger has shown in the last chapter of *The Tragic Vision*, let tension be resolved except on the aesthetic level. (And even here, on the aesthetic level, the contextualist must guard against letting aesthetic wholeness and harmony consume thematic tension.) The chaos (or "multeity") of reality must not be harmonized, complexity must not be thinned: the poem, far from reflecting metaphysical "unity in multeity," is a perilously controlled, raging cauldron of ironic thrusts and counterthrusts, of puns and ambiguities that generate mutually exclusive levels of meaning. For Coleridge, the poem sanctions not an ironic poetics and an absurdist world view, but the profound tranquillity that flows from our belief in beneficent cosmic design. In unqualified contextualism (the only kind logically possible), the poem sanctions the dread generated in our nightmare visions of an insane universe.*

---

* It is yet possible to see in Coleridge an organicism more radical even than the version postulated by recent contextualism. In *The Statesman's Manual* Coleridge makes the symbol "consubstantial" with the reality that it symbolizes as it partakes of the "unity" that it represents. Now, here, not only do we have a coalescence of imagination and nature but also a destruction of the antithesis of word and thing. This claim of "consubstantiality," grounded in absolute idealistic monism, makes quite irrelevant (1) our metaphor of the window,

The confusion of some modern scholars over the source of contextual theory would thus appear to stem from failure to take sufficient account of the world view of the chief English romantic. In conclusion, another quotation from Coleridge: the "Beautiful arises from the perceived harmony of an object, whether sight or sound, with the inborn and constitutive rules of the judgment and imagination: and it is always intuitive." [31] The real poem, for Coleridge, exists before composition in the mind; the only poem, for contextual theory, exists in language. Poetic meaning in contextual theory is identified with a unique system of linguistic relations in the poem. Poetic meaning in romantic theory is identified, not with a system of linguistic relations, but with the idealistic imagination's power to coalesce with the essence of nature.

NATURALISTIC THEORY: THE SECRETARIAL IMAGINATION

For naturalistic theory I have chosen as the metaphor of imagination the figure of the secretary because I think it suggestive of a world view polar to the idealistic conception. Generally, philosophical naturalism holds that the universe of matter is the whole universe: that it is self-existent, self-explanatory, self-operating, and self-directing. An encompassing spirit, the transcendent unification of self and world, is denied, and the totality of objects and events in space and time becomes the proper study of poet and scientist alike. The totality of truth and beauty, therefore, is

and (2) the notion that poems need to be endlessly qualified by their own internal dynamics in order to be "contextual," or utterly self-enclosed. Value and meaning fuse with the poetic context because the poetic context is all: imaginative vision, nature, and poem merge in one fluid whole. I would hesitate, however, to assign this position to Coleridge because of a certain stubborn vagueness in his claim for consubstantiality. Is the "symbol" coextensive with the poem or is it merely an object in the poem? Is the symbol a natural object or is it a linguistic construct?

20

that totality of objects and events. And because the real is fully formed, truth is independent of our perception of it, and the role of the scientist or the poet is to describe and report what he sees, and, at all costs, to limit to a minimum the intrusion of the subjective, the feelings—often a synonym for falsehood and error in naturalism.

The figure of the artist as secretary has its source in Balzac.[32] Surprisingly, however, it occurs in William Blake, too, that rhapsodic and apocalyptic voice of English romanticism, who used the very metaphor to describe the creative process. In a letter to Thomas Butts, Blake wrote: ". . . a Grand Poem. I may praise it since I dare not pretend to be any other than the secretary; the Authors are in Eternity." [33] How could this despiser of Lockean epistemology (a basis for naturalist theory of knowledge), this visionary champion of idealism, possibly make such a statement? One might suggest that, carried out to an extreme, even Coleridgean theory postulates a similar metaphor.* But Coleridge would not sanction this "carrying out" because he had deep respect for the role of language and the artist's obligation to shape it, though his idealistic position does finally undercut the fully organic role he would assign to language.

Blake is another story because he was so radical a philosophical idealist.[34] In Coleridge, I pictured his model poet using language to window the organic act of perception which reveals spirit. In Blake's theory, I would picture the model poet as an ultimate visionary who uses language (rather reluctantly) to window a world of eternality already available to him in unmediated imaginative vision.[35] In Zola, I would picture the model artist using language to window a world of natural facts that have no transcendental reference. These, in brief, are some of the similarities between

* That is, Coleridgean theory finally sees the poem as mimetic of something outside it.

the romantic and naturalistic views of poetic function which the window metaphor highlights. Now, some of the enormous differences.

The Materialistic Universe

Various elements of naturalism can be traced to the Middle Ages, and even further back to the Greeks. But for a world view that won wide acceptance among intellectuals we need only focus on the second half of the nineteenth century (and a little later on Freud), when the forces of philosophical, biological, sociological, historical, and psychological naturalism converged with conspicuously dramatic success. Much of naturalism's nineteenth-century impact is owed to its zealous propagandists, T. H. Huxley, John Tyndall, and Herbert Spencer, three who functioned particularly well as Darwin's mouthpieces. In his study of "Social Darwinism," Richard Hofstadter tells us that Huxley's American lectures "called forth the expected *odium theologicum*. 'It were bad enough to invite Huxley,' wrote one divine. 'It were better to have asked God to be present. It would have been absurd to ask them both.'" [36] And Tyndall is quoted in Jacques Barzun's *Darwin, Marx, and Wagner* as saying that "at the present moment, all our philosophy, all our poetry, all our science, all our art—Shakespeare, Newton, and Raphael—are potential in the fires of the sun." [37] We have come to expect better reactions from the enlightened clergy. As for the scientists, we expect no self-respecting inquirer to make such extravagant, such "unverifiable" claims, to use one of their favorite terms. And yet, though the propagandists have had their day, naturalistic conceptions hang on for many of us as the significant definitions of man and nature.

Much fine work has been done on the scientific and philosophical backgrounds of naturalism.[38] I wish here to recall only briefly some of the conclusions.

22

What Darwin, Marx, and Freud did, in effect, was to systematize the whole of reality at the level of observable phenomena. In a way the naturalists agreed to the romantic assertion of man's continuity with nature. The huge difference, of course, was that they accounted for man, nature, and the relationship itself materialistically. In this cold world in which communion with beneficent spirit was only fantasy, "things" were seen as the "only reality," nature was understood mechanistically, and man as a function of preexisting matter was denied creativity. Imagination (a pejorative term now), feelings, and will were all subsumed by a scheme of deterministic materialism and accounted for by positivistic method.[39] The artist who held such assumptions could be at best a secretary, at worst a slave.

As a theory of reality, then, naturalism postulates in its crudest form a despiritualized universe, and in its more sophisticated formulations takes a noncommittal attitude toward a transcendent or supermaterial reality.[40] In either formulation the physical self becomes part of the Darwinian primordial slime, while the self as a sentient perceiver stands on the edge of a yawning chasm that separates him from the inhuman force of the world of objects. No longer continuous with spirit in nature—as in romantic theory—the self is now but a discrete particular, alone and unrelated and unresolved in cosmic design and purpose. Locked in space and time, and without access to any universal currents of being, we are faced with natural facts that are simply natural facts, with a world in which the law of change or process is the law of material reality. The romantic could find objective form and value in external reality because his world of natural objects was coherent with a world of spirit. The theory of the idealistic coherence of self and nature postulated not only an objective world of value, not only a subjective creation of value and meaning, but finally a mutually creative self and

23

nature which were interdependent and interpenetrative, and, in their interpenetration, the source of all cognitive, aesthetic, and ethical value. The naturalist skirts the revolution of German idealism and, epistemologically, returns to a view of the subject-object relationship which works with Descartes's division of mind from world, and which suggests that mind is passive, that knowledge comes wholly from the impact of object (mind as secretary), and, conversely, that the subject brings no universally valid ordering categories to experience.

From whichever point of view we understand naturalism—as a theory of passive mind enclosed by a purely secular world vacated by the gods, or as a theory of biological evolution, or as a theory of psychological determinism, or even as a Marxian theory of history—the self is defined in nontranscendental terms *in* time. The image may be Locke's, Darwin's, or Freud's, but it is an image empirically and materialistically constructed. As a world view, naturalism is fully alive. Though not many of us are willing to think of it as providing the final answers to the enduring questions, and though its enthusiastic nineteenth-century formulation has been put into reasonable perspective, an expression of the romantic faith in the spiritual correspondence of subject and object no longer seems honestly possible.

In our day the naturalistic view of things has informed the existentialist's thinking. When he speaks of the "absurdity" of reality, he speaks of that abject terror that descends upon him as he contemplates a universe in which he is an alien in almost any sense of the word. Unable to validate ontological extensions of the self in nature, existential man conceives of himself as an isolated, private being whose thoughts, feelings, and, most of all, imaginative creations have only a temporary and local significance. With the dissolution of the romantic coherence of self and nature accomplished, existential man can cast but a shadow of incoherent outline on a natural world that rejects it. As Wallace Stevens put it, today's poet lives in the "world of Darwin and not in the world of Plato." [41] The transcendent self is dead.

Zola: Literature as Naturalistic Transparency

Emile Zola's long essay "The Experimental Novel" is probably the best example of a theory of literature formulated under the direct influence of a philosophically naturalistic world view. For Coleridge, the master teacher was Schelling, and poetry's context was the idealistic universe. For Zola, the master teacher was the scientist Claude Bernard, a "savant whose authority is unquestioned," [42] and fiction's context was the materialistic universe: "I'm going to try and prove . . . that if the experimental method leads to the knowledge of physical life, it should also lead to the knowledge of the passionate and intellectual life." [43] And why not, if passion and intellect are functions of matter?

Predictably, the artist becomes a kind of photographer whose observations "should be an exact representation of nature. . . . He listens to nature and he writes under its dictation." [44] Zola's rhetorical emphasis is clear: the artist is a recorder, a secretary to the world of fact. Epistemology as it was conceived in romantic theory is met by "experimental reasoning, which combats one by one the hypotheses of the idealists." [45] The study of the "abstract and metaphysical" —bad words in Zola's vocabulary—will be replaced by the "study of the natural man" [46] because the abstract and the metaphysical were characteristic of romanticism, which to Zola was the "ravings of a group of men" who believed, because they were idealists, that they possessed the "criterion of exterior things." [47] But like those "raving" poets before him, Zola gave literary art a transparent function. He felt that perfectly executed naturalistic literature would become a window to man's social condition, the improvement of which would serve a "high morality." [48] He, too, like Coleridge before him, believed that literature had much more important things to do than simply to "be" a contextual entity. In romantic theory language had to function as window to the self's transcendental transactions with an idealistic nature. In naturalistic theory language had to function as window to the self's finite transactions with a finite, deterministic nature. But in both theories, literature's highest function was its ability to give access to extraliterary value.

T. E. Hulme: Beyond Aesthetic Transparency

The word "seminal" is overworked these days, but I can think of no better way of describing T. E. Hulme's *Speculations*. Beautiful in its terseness, the book summarizes (but with polemical oversimplifications) the essential philosophical assumptions of romantic and naturalistic theory, and then anticipates with insight the development of contextual theory. Hulme can speak for himself: "One of the main achievements of the nineteenth century was the elaboration and universal application of the principle of *continuity*. The destruction of this conception is, on the contrary, an urgent necessity of the present." [49] And again: "If we . . . form a clear conception of the nature of a discontinuity, of a chasm, and form in ourselves the temper of mind which can support this opposition without irritation, we shall then have in our hands an instrument which may shatter all this confused thinking." [50] By evoking the metaphor of the continuum Hulme put his finger on the guiding conception that underlies romantic and naturalistic theories of reality. Whether or not Coleridge and Zola were "confused" thinkers, both postulated world views based on a single principle of continuous unity. It would follow that their views, by

26

being singularly comprehensive, identified value, aesthetic and cognitive, with the all-encompassing principle, be it idealistically or materialistically grounded. A poem or a novel works best within such a scheme when it allows its auditor access to that principle, that ultimate truth and value, which exists outside the aesthetic object and independent of it. Hence the metaphor of the window.

But what if our conceptions of (1) the nature of reality and (2) the nature of man's apprehension of reality are based not on the assumption of continuity, but on the assumption of *discontinuity*? What if, to put it another way, the good, the true, and the beautiful do not merge and fuse under a monistic scheme like that of Coleridge or Zola? Hulme suggests a theory close to Ernst Cassirer's epistemology of symbolic forms,[51] wherein man's various ways of apprehending reality (the poetic, the scientific, the religious, etc.) are themselves discrete functions. To give the aesthetic realm, for example, a coherence and meaning peculiar to it is to see the aesthetic realm as self-sufficient (contextual if you will), which is the way Kant wanted it in the first place, and decidedly not the way romantic or naturalistic theory saw it.

With his notion of discontinuity, and with his notions (derived from Kant and Bergson) of the uniqueness of both aesthetic intuition and language within the poetic context, Hulme opens a new line of aesthetic inquiry.* The idea that the poem, by definition, is itself a self-enclosed, self-sufficient, and organic entity throws out its transparency function. Historically, Hulme stands about midway between Poe and Baudelaire, who were anticipators of the symbolist aesthetic, and those modern contextualist critics who derive some of their

* Though Hulme opens the door to contextualist theory, he is not himself a contextualist. Hulme's intensive manifolds become autonomous and autotelic images in poems; they are not themselves self-sufficient poems.

27

leading ideas not from romantic but from symbolist theory.

SYMBOLIST THEORY: THE MAGICAL IMAGINATION

Symbolism is the effort to create poetry outside romantic or naturalistic aesthetics. By anchoring himself in the naturalist's materialistic universe, the symbolist poet rejects Schelling's version of the coherence of imagination and reality (which necessitates an idealistic transparency of the poetic object), but he will not accept the naturalist's secretarial imagination either (which necessitates a materialistic transparency). His ideal for poetry is not transparency, but opacity. If a poem is to exist opaquely, for itself alone, then the role of language must be reconceived. As long as language is seen as "form," a window to "content" which exists independently of language, then a form-content split is unavoidable.

Operating in a paradoxical situation (rejecting, that is, romantic theories of reality and poetic value, but unable to accept all the naturalistic alternatives), a symbolist poet seeks, while working within an alien materialistic context, to establish a new theory of poetic value based on the idea of the organicity of the poem itself. His thinking might go something like this: A poem's content resides in the verbal medium alone; a poem's "ideas" or "meanings" are realized only while the imagination is working in language. Therefore, form and content are indissoluble, quite literally, since to change even one word (form) is to change, however slightly, the idea (content). The window of language has been painted. I have chosen the word "constructive" to describe such a theory of imagination because the poem is literally a created entity, an utterly new thing in nature, itself organic. When the symbolists theorize in contextual terms, they are more accurately the inheritors of Kantian aesthetics than are the romantics

28

(whom they are supposed to follow), since they postulate the complete autonomy of the aesthetic realm.

The following passage from Kant's *Critique of Aesthetic Judgment* is the germinal source of the constructive imagination and of modern contextualism:

> . . . by an aesthetical Idea I understand that representation of the Imagination which occasions much thought without, however, any definite thought, i.e. any *concept*, being capable of being adequate to it; it consequently cannot be completely compassed and made intelligible by language. . . . The Imagination . . . is very powerful in creating another nature, as it were, out of the material that actual nature gives it.[52]

As the contextualists read this passage, the poetic object is an organic affair, a closed system of linguistic relations, a verbal universe, a "nature," whose meaning cannot be translated for the reason that it inheres in the peculiar context or formal structure of the poem itself. The imagination that brings this unique world of meaning into being is said to be constructive— literally "creative"—and autonomous. The autonomous literary imagination, bound to the medium in which it chooses to express itself, makes meaning *in* the medium. Language ceases to function as transparent form through which we are given access to meaning and value. The poem, by being autotelic, becomes opaque.

But to identify symbolist and contextualist theory on a one-to-one basis would be a gross distortion of literary history. For though the core motivation of a symbolist may be toward a theory of poetic autonomy, other elements of his aesthetic militate against it, and in fact suggest a transparency of poetic form. Over and over again, Poe and Mallarmé speak of aesthetic beauty with a capital *B*, and it is clear that they are speaking of a realm outside space and time. Since, however, spirit and nature are not continuous in a materialistic universe, the symbolist, in an effort to reach spirit, often invokes the analogy of magic. Poetry is incantation, and the poet's weird abracadabra becomes a window to an occult realm that exists beyond the frontiers of a materialistic universe.[53] I have decided on "magical" to describe such a view of the poetic imagination.

There is a hint of the magical theory of poetry in Poe's "Letter to B____":

> Think of poetry, dear B____, think of poetry, and then think of—Dr. Samuel Johnson! Think of all that is aery and fairy-like, and then of all that is hideous and unwieldy; think of his huge bulk, the Elephant! and then—and then think of the Tempest—the Mid-summer Night's Dream—Prospero —Oberon—and Titania! [54]

Poe as Prospero the magician—hating the gravitational pull of an ugly world of things which Samuel Johnson, fat and unmoveable, had proved existed by kicking a stone—takes the flight of Ariel into the gossamer realms of magic and fairies.* Natural analogy does not suffice,[55] now, because nature is a symbol of nothing in a materialistic universe. The poet as magician will use natural images, but only after they have been dislocated from the empirical order of things and mixed in the alchemical alembic of the imagination. The strange concoction that emerges will be a poem *"through"* which (as a window) "we attain . . . but brief and indeterminate glimpses" [56] of a realm of "supernal Beauty" [57] which exists, as Poe characteristically wrote in his "Dream-Land," "Out of Space—out of Time." [58] The magical imagination vaults over nature, and language once more becomes a foyer, an opening through which we are given value and meaning that exists independent of the poem itself.

---

* For the "Ariel" and "gravity" metaphors I am indebted to two papers by Murray Krieger, "Northrop Frye and Contemporary Criticism: Ariel and the Spirit of Gravity" and "The Existential Basis of Contextual Criticism," now conveniently reprinted in his *The Play and Place of Criticism* (Baltimore, 1967).

Below I try to distinguish the contextual and magical views in my illustrations of Poe, Baudelaire, Mallarmé, and Valéry. The four poets hold together, I feel, because of their intense desire to establish a self-sufficient *raison d'être* for poetry. Whenever they speak theoretically, they tend to speak for the singular uniqueness of poetry, despite the contradictions. Valéry comes closest to articulating a contextual poetics; Poe, with a foot in each world, speaks of both transparency and opacity.

Poe and Baudelaire: Magical Transparency versus Contextual Opacity

In a few essays, Poe touched on the major ideas in symbolist poetics. Early in his brief career, in the "Letter to B____" (1831), he consciously set out to establish a basis for poetry outside the theories of Wordsworth and Coleridge. The "Lake School," he thought, was responsible for formulating a "most singular heresy": that the "end of poetry is, or should be, instruction." [50] Realizing that the "instruction" of a Wordsworth or a Coleridge was not simply easy moralizing, and that the great romantics were immersed in idealistic philosophy, Poe yet felt that philosophical poetry, no matter how sophisticated, still functioned as a handmaiden. He found the *Biographia Literaria* badly flawed; it was a shame, he thought, "that such a mind" as Coleridge's "should be buried in metaphysics." [60] As for Wordsworth, Poe had "no faith in him." [61] This is not Poe the hatchet man here; his argument is a technical one centered on the workings of the creative process: ". . . the difference, then, with which I venture to dispute their [Wordsworth's and Coleridge's] authority, would be overwhelming, did I not feel, from the bottom of my heart, that learning has little to do with the imagination." [62]

Poe thus parted with the English romantics on the question of the poetic imagination's function. The idealistic coherence of imagination and reality in spirit seemed (to Poe) to rob poetry of its own integrity. If the romantic poet was at once reaching from and into spirit, and spirit was the identity of beauty, truth, and goodness, then the poem itself was a window, and, as such, not truly self-sufficient. So, apparently following Kant's theory of autonomy which Coleridge never seemed to abjure, Poe made the imagination autonomous by sectioning mind into three discrete compartments: moral sense, intellect, and imagination or taste. Through the imagination alone beauty with a capital *B* was reached.[63] And here is the problem. It is simply not enough to make the imagination autonomous, or to isolate the aesthetic realm from the ethical and the cognitive. As long as that aesthetic realm remains beyond space and time—"a beauty which is not afforded the soul by any existing collocation of earth's forms" [64] —it cannot be wholly contained within the medium. It takes a "wild effort to reach the beauty above," [65] wrote Poe; therefore the poem's function is a transparent one, and the autonomy of the poem itself is defeated. On occasion he demanded that the poem be "written solely for the poem's sake," and that the critic comment upon the work of art only as a work of art, not as a part of history—literary, philosophical, political, or otherwise. We have heard this many times from contextual critics, and we are justified in saying that this last aspect of Poe's work anticipates much of modern criticism.[66] Only this aspect, however.

Turning from Poe to Baudelaire is like turning to Poe again. But to see Poe through Baudelaire's eyes is to see him from an amazingly enthusiastic and brilliant point of view. It is difficult to overstate Baudelaire's respect for Poe when he himself wrote: "I should willingly say of him and of a special class of men what the catechism says of our Lord: 'He has suffered much for us.' " [67] Luckily, Baudelaire did not simply worship

Poe as an aesthetic Christ, but also studied him carefully, and expanded his notions into many of the significant positions within a symbolist aesthetic.

When Baudelaire wrote his essays on Poe in the 1850's and 1860's the utilitarian view of art held wide credence.[68] As a forerunner of contextualism, Baudelaire fought against utilitarianism, and in Poe he found an ally:

> For a long time there has been a utilitarian movement in the United States which seeks to carry poetry along with it like everything else. There are humanitarian poets, poets who favor women's suffrage, poets opposed to the tax on cereals, and poets who wish to build workhouses. I swear that I am not referring to people in France. It is not my fault if the same disputes and the same theories agitate different countries. In his lectures Poe declared war on all that.[69]

Though he starts with a strong nonutilitarian propensity, Baudelaire undercuts his implicit contextual ideas when he pursues Poe's theory of the imagination as a faculty capable of magically transcending the materialistic universe. Like Poe before him he could not see spirit as coinstantaneous with nature and the perceiving self. In the romantic theory of Coleridge, spirit, the transcendent meaning of poetry, was the continuum of self and nature, the matrix of the natural world. But in magical symbolist theory the occult world the poet seeks to evoke has no place in the structure of his materialistic universe. The magical imagination is therefore assigned (by Baudelaire) the power of breaking beyond a finite materialistic universe, beyond insufficient natural analogy, into a realm that it alone can penetrate.[70] As a would-be contextual theorist of the imagination, Baudelaire has the same trouble that Poe had. For by placing the aesthetic realm outside the poem, he forces the poem itself to function transparently; this occurs despite his effort, like Poe's, to re-

33

vamp practical criticism along lines that remind us of recent contextual practice.[71]

There is a part of Poe which takes us more steadily in contextual directions. Poe the craftsman, the author of the "The Philosophy of Composition," implied somewhat contradictorily that only in the language of poetry could the beauty "above" be reached.* This becomes the ever-expanding theme in symbolist theory as we move toward Valéry. When the "above" drops out, when the poetic imagination as well as the poet is bound in space and time, the aesthetic realm becomes surrounded and contained by the verbal medium. Then, in the agnostic, naturalistic universe of Darwin or Marx, the poem itself becomes the self-enclosed creation of the constructive imagination. Baudelaire noticed that despite Poe's "bold and roving imagination" he was a superb technician. His style, Baudelaire felt, was pure and "always correct."[72] But perhaps Baudelaire's most suggestive comment on the contextual side of Poe is this one: "construction, the armature, . . . is the most important guarantee of the mysterious life of the works of the mind."[73] The obsessive insistence on craft in Poe and Baudelaire is more than the universal concern of the artist for his medium; it is a gesture, as Charles Feidelson pointed out,[74] toward the idea that in the medium, and only in the medium, does poetic value reside. From here it is but a small step to the more advanced notion that symbolism is achieved solely in poetic context. In a critical essay not on Poe, Baudelaire summarized those symbolist ideas that come closest to modern theory when he wrote that "Nature is ugly" and therefore no longer a ground of value, and thus what he labeled the *Constructive* imagination" brings into "being" a "world."[75] The terminology is sometimes archaic and the ideas contradictory, but a substantial part of Poe and Baudelaire

* Poe is an affectivist whose overwhelming theoretical interest is in the response, not in the work itself. What I choose to stress here is that in Poe which attracted the French symbolists.

34

ought to remind us of the emphasis of the New Criticism.

SYMBOLIST THEORY: THE CONSTRUCTIVE IMAGINATION

Mallarmé and Valéry

Mallarmé once claimed that he "learned English simply in order to read Poe better"; [76] certainly he learned from Baudelaire. Like his masters, he found that he had to reject romanticism and naturalism, and in some of his more important essays he concentrated on the problem of formulating a symbolist theory of language. But in "The Evolution of Literature" he set down his criticism of his theoretical inheritance. He accepted, first of all, the idea of the alien fragmented and discontinuous universe, which had a direct bearing on the fate of romantic idealism. No longer, he thought, was there a possibility of an Emersonian representative poetic self: "We are now witnessing a spectacle . . . which is truly extraordinary, unique in the history of poetry: every poet is going off by himself with his own flute, and playing the song he pleases." [77] Literature became, in his postromantic era, a private and "entirely . . . individual matter." [78] The naturalistic view of poetry was even more unacceptable to him. Mallarmé is humorously arrogant about naturalistic writing: ". . . there is the same difference between that and poetry as there is between a corset and a beautiful throat." [79]

His salient contribution to a symbolist view of poetry from my perspective was his effort to establish the poem as a contextual entity with substantive status in a language purified, or emptied, of all external reference. Mallarmé's belief in the organic wholeness of poetry places him solidly in the Kantian tradition, but there is a contradiction in his thinking because his views of the poetic faculty are unquestionably colored

35

idea of magic. This strain of magical trans-
~y, this realm of pure beauty which he often re-
:d to as the "occult," [80] is called a "reality," but it
 "exist . . . [only] on a piece of paper." [81] In one
breath, almost, Mallarmé collects the conflicting elements within nineteenth-century symbolist theory.

Perhaps the one word he used most frequently to
characterize what the symbolist feels to be peculiarly
the context of poetry is "immaculate." [82] By it he suggests the theory that the language of poetry is purged
by the imagination of all those transparent elements,
those symbolic characters that lead us outside context
to the empirical world, or things as they are. The "immaculate" language of symbolist poetry is in its reference neither objective (it does not point to external
reality) nor subjective (it is not an expressive outpour-
ing). The poem conceived as immaculate "symbol"
exists as all imaginative literature should, in Mallarmé's opinion, alone and all exclusively." [83] Marshal-
ing an argument that is now typical of neo-Kantian
theory, he anticipates Philip Wheelwright's theory of
language outlined in *The Burning Fountain* by making
poetic metaphor constitutive of the verbal cosmos of
the poem: "The poet must establish a careful relationship between two images, from which a third element,
clear and fusible, will be distilled and caught by our
imagination." [84] The ideal poem, as Mallarmé put it, is
a "reasonable number of words stretched beneath our
mastering glance, arranged in enduring figures, and
followed by silence." [85] In that poem of "enduring figures," the poet "disappears," his voice is "stilled," and
the words of the poem taken together fashion a "single
new word which is total in itself and foreign to the
language" of the world of "action." [86] The "inner
structures of a book of verse," its totality of import, are
"inborn." [87] In the framework of his thought, however,
Mallarmé's ideas on language were as often grounded
in magical transparency as they were in contextual

36

opacity. Hence, the poem either facilitates a magical transcendence through a "kind of incantation" [88] or it evokes nothing beyond itself, but rather, through its concrete, self-sufficient, linguistic figurations emanating from a constructive and autonomous imagination, achieves its own end.

The line runs from Poe to Valéry, as Eliot has noticed, but by the time we get to Valéry, the magical temptations have been purged from the symbolist aesthetic. Valéry outlines an aesthetic on a completely nontransparent basis: the linguistic medium is the beginning and end of poetry. In his own reading of literary history, he saw poets in reaction to romanticism becoming increasingly more interested in technical perfection. The turning point, he thought, was Poe. For Poe, unlike many of the greatest writers, did not "combine the materials of discursive or empirical knowledge with the creations of the inner being." [89] Valéry's understanding of Poe's attempt to set poetry on a contextual base was expressed best when he wrote that Poe tried to unite "mathematics with mysticism," which is a way of suggesting that Poe's interest in precision and technique led him to seek linguistic enclosure of the aesthetic realm.[90]

Valéry's emphasis is heavily semantic. For those who would identify the whole import of symbolist theory with a disguised romantic idealism, or with magic, he is the principal barrier. In line with American contextualists, he divides language into the pragmatic (transparent) and poetic (opaque) functions. For Valéry the pragmatic function of language usually coincides with general usage because it is purposefully utilitarian and referential. In this function words are significant only as counters, and only insofar as the counters are clearly signs that take us outside themselves to a meaning. According to philosophical naturalism and recent logical positivism, this is the main function of language. But for Valéry there is another function in which language achieves, ideally, a "perfect uselessness." To use his famous term, it becomes "pure," and pure language, like Mallarmé's "immaculate" language, is not a window to anything.[91]

Valéry summarized succinctly the main movement of aesthetic inquiry since Poe when he wrote: "No doubt the product [poem] is the thing that lasts and has, or should have, a meaning of itself and an independent existence."[92] The poet's task is "to create a world or order of things, a system of relations unconnected with the practical order."[93] He concludes that the world of the poem is complete and "solely verbal."[94] But what about the new order created by the poem? Valéry's answer will stump those who wish to see all symbolist poetry as incantation: "X . . . would like one to believe that a metaphor is a communication from heaven. A metaphor is *what happens* when one *looks in a certain way*."[95] Thus, though metaphor may compose this organic world of the symbolist poem, neither the metaphor nor the poem is in any way a transcendental springboard. The poem exists in the world of Darwin, not in the world of Plato or Emerson; Stevens said it, but Valéry might have. Finally, all those interested in the theory of symbolist poetry, according to Valéry, work toward a "kind of verbal materialism." "You can *look down* on novelists, philosophers, and all who are enslaved to words by credulity—who *must* believe that their speech is real by its content and signifies some reality. But as for you, you know that the reality of a discourse is only the words and the poems."[96] Poetry has been given unique being, or, as a philosopher might put it, ontological status. And this it never had before.

3

The Explicit Poetics of W. B. Yeats

POSSIBLY the most innocently perceptive comment ever made about W. B. Yeats's early career was made by Yeats himself when he wrote, "I was always discovering places where I would like to spend my whole life."[1] His statement suggests that he never actually settled upon one systematic, logically controlled interest in a single poetic, but rather had a hunger for any number, some of which, it turns out, were mutually exclusive. But he rarely cared about logical coherence. His was a search for effectiveness of poetic statement, and the record of his poetry is evidence enough that he found it. In this chapter I want to do with Yeats's prose what has not been done before: to analyze and coordinate all the significant strands of it by asking two of the central questions posed in literary theory: What are the nature of the poetic faculty and the reality within which it must function? What are the nature and the value of the poetic object?

We often forget that Yeats was already thirty-five years old in 1900, and that he grew up and produced what would be for most writers a sizeable amount of work in an age he felt to be dominated by naturalistic thought. Unlike some of the more effete and (from his own testimony) rather mindless members of the Rhymers' Club, those English aesthetes who weakly counterparted the French symbolist poets, Yeats could not, in the 1890's, rest with the creation of escapist poetry alone. He had to think about what he was doing, and, because of historical circumstances, to be an apologist as well.[2] My chronicle begins with his ambiguous reactions toward science and spiritualism; it continues with his excursions into romantic and symbolist theory, then with the poetics of will and impersonality, and, finally, the philosophy—if that is not too grand a word for so unsystematic a mind—of immersion in history. I am not trying to demonstrate that he developed through three or four or eight stages, for I think the frames of his thought were outlined very early.[3] And if in his beginning we see him discovering various paradises of the imagination, we also see him discriminating among them through subtlety of emphasis. He found that he could not be everywhere at once—that, in fact, he never wanted to be.

IDEAS OF GOOD AND EVIL: YEATS'S THEORETICAL INHERITANCE [4]

In a letter dated May 15, 1903, Yeats wrote to an Irish-American friend, John Quinn: "Tomorrow I shall send you my new book, *Ideas of Good and Evil*. I feel that much of it is out of my present mood; that it is true, but no longer true for me." [5] For the sake of historical "truth," one wishes that Yeats had gone on to explain exactly what was no longer true. But he did not, and we must content ouselves with critical analysis without authorial guidance. I think that when we examine his whole career as critic we will agree with him that something had gone stale in *Ideas of Good and Evil*. Very briefly, the elements of his revolt against the aesthetic and bald spiritualist doctrines of *Ideas of Good and Evil* were already implicit in much that he had written and experienced in the years preceding the publication of his first significant book of criticism.

Ideas of Good and Evil is an assertion of poetic theory informed by a need for transcendence. Growing up

40

in a period when science seemed to be cutting the
heart out of the poetic imagination undoubtedly
helped to shape Yeats into the rebel that he was. The
age did not make him a great poet, but it forced him
into apologetics. For example, what more necessary
time could there be to assert the inviolable integrity of
poetry than at the close of the nineteenth century,
when poetry's unique value was being seriously ques-
tioned and, some thought, destroyed? What better
time could there be to assert a creative view of mind
than when mind was denied creativity by the unlovely
alliance between science and literary realism? And,
what better time to assume the power of the supernatural than in an era of scientific thought, when the supernatural was denied with so much unscientific enthusiasm and absoluteness? Yeats suggests his crisis
when he wrote in his *Autobiography* that his "father's
unbelief had set [him] thinking," because he "did not
think that he could live without religion." [6] Even a
casual reading of the *Autobiography* reveals that
among the major themes in the book, probably the
most consistently reiterated is the cursing of Huxley,
Tyndall, Locke, Zola, and Marx, the "hot-faced money
changers" and those clever rhetoricians, the journal-
ists.[7] Yeats's heroes are Kant, Berkeley, Swedenborg,
the French symbolists, and the Irish aristocrats: a mot-
ley crew when mixed in with Yeats's magic makers,
Madame Blavatsky and MacGregor Mathers. The categories of opposition are melodramatically formulated.
The contest *is* between good and evil. But this account
is not quite accurate in itself, though it is a traditional
view of his early career. For every idea that attracted
him also repelled, and every idea that repelled him
also attracted. Total rejection or total commitment to a
philosophical position is not the response typical of
Yeats. The twists and turns of his career were the symbolic maneuvers of a man too honest and complex to
see reality in any simple way, too much aware of his

own ambiguous and contradictory motivations to deny one of them in order to assert another. To use a familiar Yeatsian term, it is not a question of choosing one half of an antinomy or the other, but a question of wanting both at once.

An unexpected example of Yeatsian ambiguity (likely unintended) is the essay "Magic" (1901), in which he lists the main principles of occultist doctrine:

> (1) That the borders of our mind are ever shifting, and that many minds can flow into one another. . . . (2) That the borders of our memories are as shifting, and that our memories are a part of one great memory, the memory of Nature herself. (3) That this great mind and great memory can be evoked by symbols.[8]

Implied here is a theory of cosmic continuity, but much of the essay is informed by a particular analogy: poet is to poem as magician is to magic. The magical conception of the poet, a familiar one in French symbolist aesthetics, is based on the assumption that, as Baudelaire said, "Nature is ugly"; that, in philosophical terms, nature is not spiritually coherent and continuous with the perceiving imagination; that the subject-object division is an overpowering one. Language in the alembic of the magical imagination becomes incantatory force which propels the poet out of a materialistic universe. The poet, in Yeats's words, taps the powers of a transcendent "supernatural artist" who vitalizes the poem.[9] This is not a Coleridgean, idealistic theory of poetry. The poet as romantic, on the contrary, had seen himself benevolently located within a natural world coherent with spirit. The romantic postulated a poetic wherein organic nature, a symbol of spirit, was the norm, while the magical symbolist postulated a poetic wherein nature is a symbol of nothing, and thus must be imaginatively transcended. The two theories of poetry are not so neatly distinguished in Yeats's essay. Though in his three principles he postulates romantic continuity, later he postulates discontinuity: ". . . we must cry out that imagination is always seeking to remake the world according to the impulses and the patterns in that Great Mind. . . ." [10] Far from reflecting a romantic point of view, Yeats implies here a universe so alien that the poetic imagination seeks to become as literally transcendent as it is constructive. When the planes of material process are not intersected by the planes of spiritual stasis, then the magician must somehow fix his vision through the alchemy of art. Nature fails the symbolist and the imagination must go it alone.

Whatever confusion or vacillation one might detect in Yeat's theory of poetry as it is presented in "Magic," there is little doubt that at that time he was seeking a way out of the cold, materialistic reality so frighteningly described to him by science. He required a second world, whether or not he could decide on the position to assign it in his scheme. In an often-quoted letter to Katherine Tynan, he said of his early poetry: "It is almost all a flight into fairyland from the real world, and a summons to that flight. . . . It is not a poetry of insight and knowledge, but of longing and complaint —the cry of the heart against necessity." [11] It is common to read that Yeats's involvements with the spiritualists and the Cabalists implied a rejection of the naturalistic account of reality, but his deterministic characterization of the empirical world as "necessity" suggests that he was shaped by what he so detested. Despite the number of studies that begin with the assumption that Yeats swallowed much of the occult traditions and the philosophical idealism to which he exposed himself, the question of his own belief is still substantially open.

It would not be difficult to marshal evidence supporting the contention that Yeats was a doctrinal poet of the occult, nor would it be very difficult to footnote an argument supporting the opposite contention.

43

What I emphasize here is that ambiguous vein in his work, grounded in the comic gesture and skepticism, which makes an airtight doctrinal or antidoctrinal argument quite impossible. Again, letters to Katherine Tynan are relevant. Twice in 1888 he wrote to her in a tone that, if we hold he is a wholehearted believer, is very curious: "A sad accident happened at Madame Blavatsky's lately, I hear. A big materialist sat on the astral double of a poor young Indian. It was sitting on the sofa and he was too material to be able to see it. Certainly a sad accident!" [12] If this sounds like the cynical and detached ironist, a letter written a few months later reveals Yeats as the strangely defensive and embarrassed apologist:

> I am to write a series of articles on the difference between Scotch and Irish fairies for some new paper. . . . I must be careful in no way to suggest that fairies, or something like them, do veritably exist, some flux and flow between man and the unresolvable mystery. . . . I am going to tell you of a spiritualistic story. Do not be angry! I tell it because it is pretty.[13]

The contours of Yeats's belief in the period before publication of *Ideas of Good and Evil* may be studied further in his accounts of his early life in the *Autobiography*. The relevant sections are the first three: "Reveries over Childhood," "The Trembling of the Veil," and "Dramatis Personae." Hazard Adams' idea that the *Autobiography* and even *A Vision* are "books in themselves," imaginative realizations rather than simply "mines of interpretation situated somewhere underneath the poetry," is a cogent warning, and his suggestion of a comic tone is an illumination.[14] Adams' theories about the two books are vindicated if we read them as we would a long work of fiction: not for isolated statement of belief, but for the development of pattern and tone indicative of formally achieved intention. I believe the tone of the *Autobiography* is characterized most saliently by its doubleness, and that its major manifestation is in those passages describing Yeats's introductions to occultism.

As Jacques Barzun has pointed out, spiritualism was a reaction against the naturalism of the later nineteenth century.[15] On philosophical grounds spiritualism denied the exclusiveness of empiricist epistemology. Yeats suggests that his own spiritualistic interests were similarly motivated:

> It was only when I began to study psychical research and mystical philosophy that I broke away from my father's influence. He had been a follower of John Stuart Mill. . . . But through this new research, this reaction from popular science, I had begun to feel that I had allies for my secret thought.[16]

That "secret thought," however, is not necessarily the same as "psychical research" and "mystical philosophy." Allies are not always brothers, and neither are they always committed to the same thing. The difficulty in defining Yeats's exact attitude lies in his simultaneous detachment and commitment. For example, of his Hermetic Society friends he wrote: "We spent a good deal of time in the Kildare Street Museum passing our hands over the glass cases, *feeling or believing we felt* the Odic Force flowing from the big crystals." [17]

Yeats described the young Hermeticists as "thirsty." No question about it, he was thirsty, too. And yet the stories he told about them were often half humorous, ironic, and delivered with his fine sense of comic timing:

> My friend had written to some missionary society to send him to the South Seas, when I offered him Renan's *Life of Christ* and a copy of *Esoteric Buddhism*. He refused both, but a few days later while reading for an examination in Kildare Street Library, he asked in an idle moment for *Esoteric Buddhism* and came out an esoteric Buddhist.[18]

45

The great danger, Yeats knew, lay in the despair of naturalism and the all too easy way out offered by the other extreme. There he and his friends were, at the close of the nineteenth century, believing in the special efficacy of poetic vision and seeing it denied all around them. Any way around the problem might seem a good way, especially if there was a gesture in the direction of philosophy to add respectability. Yeats tells this story of a convert to occultism: "I found him [a fellow Hermeticist] a day later in much depression. I said, 'Did he refuse to listen to you?' 'Not at all,' was the answer, 'for I had only been talking for a quarter of an hour when he said he believed.' " [19]

Humor in the *Autobiography* is generally the chief distancing technique, and humorous sexual allusion is the punctuating motif of a long section presenting his initial impressions of Madame Blavatsky and Mac-Gregor Mathers. Yeats's later poetry is laden with images of the sensual, and, particularly in the "Crazy Jane" poems, it is marked by a joyous elevation of sexual experience. Concomitantly, the later work exhibits an apparent disavowal of those exclusive supernatural obsessions, that part of Yeats which wanted to turn away from the body and an unsatisfactory world. Judging from his accounts of the spiritualists in the *Autobiography*, the later, wicked old man was not a new man. If his selection of the sexual detail points the erotic frustrations of the thwarted self turning toward God, the same selection further strengthens the Yeatsian vision that strings a man between two equally powerful principles: in the *Autobiography*, the antinomy of self and soul.

> I noticed a handsome clever woman of the world there, who seemed certainly very much out of place, penitent though she thought herself. Presently there was much scandal and gossip for the penitent was plainly entangled with two young men, who were expected to grow into ascetic

sages. The scandal was so great that Madame Blavatsky had to call the penitent before her and speak after this fashion, "We think that it is necessary to crush the animal nature; you should live in chastity in act and thought. Initiation is granted only to those who are entirely chaste," but after some minutes in that vehement style, the penitent standing crushed and shamed before her, "I cannot permit you more than one." She was quite sincere but thought that nothing mattered but what happened in the mind, and that if we could not master the mind our actions were of little importance.[20]

Despite Yeats's wish that Madame Blavatsky boost him over the apparently insurmountable walls of scientific thought to "communing with God only,"[21] his awareness of ironic incongruity within the spiritualist experience is not the stamp of a mind immersed in mystical perception. I suppose I could put it very simply by saying that sex mattered to Yeats, though it had nothing to do with idealistic epistemology. Even Madame Blavatsky seemed to realize that among her more dubious pupils were those who came "to listen and to turn every doctrine into a new sanction for the puritanical convictions of their Victorian childhood." And, as Yeats wittily noted, the "cranks came from half Europe and all America." There was a woman who talked perpetually of " 'the divine spark' within her, until Madame Blavatsky stopped her with—'Yes, my dear, you have a divine spark within you and if you are not careful you will hear it snore.' "[22]

However much Yeats disliked the naturalists, they had left their marks on him. It was not the esoteric Buddhist, but the Huxleyan, who after a séance "began a series of experiments" to test the validity of his experience. Yeats was a dispassionate outsider and he knew it: "A certain fanatical hungry face had been noticed red and tearful and it was quite plain that I was not in

47

agreement with their methods or their philosophy." [23]
I am not suggesting that he was merely flirting with
the exotic because he had nothing better to do. There
is no question that he too was looking for a way out of
a philosophy that reduced the contents of mind to empirical data and a way out of a world deserted by God.
That he was quick to recognize fakery, however; that
his assessment of Mathers is guarded and skeptical; [24]
that he could see, at once, the poignancy and sickness
of the "fanatical hungry face"; that he did not care, in
short, to push finite human experience away from the
center of his awareness—all these concerns shift the
question of belief to new ground. The formal statement of Yeats's "mythology" would not come until
1925 with the publication of *A Vision*. What he wrote
in that book would befuddle spiritualist and naturalist
alike. Yet it was not a new statement by any means;
very early he began to see that extremes of belief unavoidably tyrannized the poetic imagination. A slave
to the realm of spirit was no less a slave than the secretary to the realm of matter.

The problem of occultist belief is closely related to
the pressing aesthetic questions that Yeats posed and
felt he had not satisfactorily answered in *Ideas of Good
and Evil*. Not long after he published the book he
began to think that it did not truly reflect the direction
of his thought. Implicit in his accounts of occultism in
the *Autobiography* is the portrait of a man whose
needs are too complex to be met by the driving other-
worldliness of spiritualist doctrine. The mind that
communed with God alone could not focus on the
mire. Yet, the dominant aesthetic of *Ideas of Good and
Evil* is both romantic and magically symbolistic. As
Yeats formulates his aesthetic in this collection, it reflects the spiritualists' disregard of the finite—their ultimate exaltation of transcendent vision over language
and communication—and not the poet's commitment
to a "preposterous pig of a world" and painstaking

48

craft. The author of *Ideas of Good and Evil* could just as easily have applied his criticism of George Russell (AE), the mystical poet, to himself: "I sometimes wonder what he would have been had he not met in early life the poetry of Emerson and Walt Whitman, writers who have begun to seem artificial precisely because they lack the Vision of Evil." [25] The import of a "vision of evil," and of a world that could not be explained as an extension of God's being, amounts to nothing less than his most cogent criticism of romantic poetics, a criticism subtly implicit in his early literary essays.

Motivating *Ideas of Good and Evil* is the need to escape naturalist conceptions of reality and art, and its leitmotif, like that of the *Autobiography*, is a railing against the "Huxley, Tyndall, Carolus Duran, Bastien-Lepage rookery." [26] Yeats's antipathy to naturalism is, however, about the only consistently unifying theme in the book, and many of the pieces slip into vagueness and contradiction. If the essay on "Magic" only faintly mirrored his vacillation between theories of cosmic continuity and cosmic discontinuity, the essays more basically rooted in artistic concerns are dramatically divided between the necessity of craft and the necessity of transcendence.

In the most complexly suggestive of those essays, "Symbolism in Painting" (1898), Yeats is primarily concerned with the distinction, by now a commonplace, between allegory and symbol. His view of symbol here is Blakean in its feelings: "It is only a very modern Dictionary that calls a symbol 'the sign or representation of any moral thing by the image or properties of natural things,' which, though an imperfect definition, is not unlike 'The things below are as the things above' of the Emerald Tablet of Hermes!" [27] In this postulation of a romantic universe—an empirical reality emblematic of a spiritual reality—and a view of symbol as window to that relationship, Yeats is insist-

49

ing upon an idealistic view of the aesthetic object and aesthetic value. Then, calling again on the authority of Blake, he states a more radical romantic theory of poetry, this time emphasizing the power of visionary imagination to penetrate ultimate being: "William Blake has written, 'Vision or imagination'—meaning symbolism by these words—'is a representation of what actually exists, really or unchangeably.'" [28] This theory of poetry and the poetic process, wherein symbolism is equated with vision and vision is mediated by neither language nor nature, makes poetry transparent: poet and poem look into a world of essence.

In the same essay, however, Yeats offers another definition of symbolism, this one based on very different philosophical assumptions:

> All art that is not mere story-telling, or mere portraiture, is symbolic, and has the purpose of those symbolic talismans which mediaeval magicians made with complex colours and forms, and bade their patients ponder over daily, and guard with holy secrecy; for it entangles, in complex colours and forms, a part of the Divine Essence.[29]

In a concentrated summary, he formulates a symbolist poetic as magical transformation, with the poet as a consciously artful magician who has a respect for the necessary role of craft foreign to extreme idealistic theory. Implied in his statement is a view of nature as alien rather than coherent with the poetic mind. Unfortunately, Yeats has thereby clouded the issue rather than clarified it because now the poetic imagination has the double and difficult role of (1) breaking beyond the material world which is void of spirit; and yet (2) grounding itself in language if it is to construct that pure and incantatory magical symbol that is supposed to facilitate transcendence. Yeats would learn that the obsessions of transcendence often undercut the obsessions of craft. Again, like his version of romantic theory, the need to get beyond naturalistic transparency (a poem is a window to a world of dead empirical objects) has led Yeats to a conception of poetry which would finally take him beyond time. He has reinstated a unique value for poetry, to be sure, but with such vengeance that the poem is tied no longer either to nature or to an artistic medium. Instead of giving the poetic medium the self-contained value that would save it from the Huxleys and the Tyndalls, Yeats makes it a window through which the reader may view an occult spiritual world.

Yeats concluded "Symbolism in Painting" with remarks that foreshadow his later position: "The systematic mystic is not the greatest of artists, because his imagination is too great to be bounded by a picture or a song. . . . so august a beauty moves before the mind that they forget the things which move before the eyes." [30] The artist as either romantic or magic-making symbolist tends to become one among other "religious and visionary people, monks and nuns, and medicine-men and opium-eaters" [31] as he turns away from the finite, away from nature and his medium in his transcendent perception. When Yeats says that the romantic or magical imagination is "too great to be bounded by a picture or a song" he is, as poet, leaning back toward a view of the poem as an opaque entity, and to the world of time wherein the artist becomes a spiritually limited maker of poems, not a mystical seer.

"The Symbolism of Poetry" (1900) is as deeply divided between unrestrained transcendentalism and craftsmanship as "Symbolism in Painting." Again, Yeats saw symbolism as a theory of poetry which sought explicitly to counter and discredit the "scientific movement . . . which was always tending to lose itself in externalities of all kinds, in opinion, in declamation, in picturesque writing. . . ." [32] Because what disturbed him about naturalism was its reduction of all human creativity to deterministic external force, Yeats stressed in his summary of symbolism the constructive and substantive powers of poetic language, and the intransitive or self-enclosed character of the aesthetic experience: ". . . an emotion does not exist, or does not become perceptible and active among us, till it has found its expression, in colour or in sound or in form, or in all of these, and because no two modulations or arrangements of these evoke the same emotion. . . ." [33] This view of the aesthetic object as an autotelic construct, as a realm of being achieved only through careful and calculated craftsmanship, is paralleled by an appropriate description of the aesthetic experience: "The purpose of rhythm . . . is to prolong the moment of contemplation, . . . to keep us in that state of perhaps real trance, in which the mind liberated from the pressure of the will is unfolded in symbols." [34] Or, in the same vein, "I would have been like one who does not know that he is passing through a wood because his eyes are on the pathway." [35] I have used the word "intransitive" to describe this view of the aesthetic experience, borrowing it from Eliseo Vivas, a modern contextualist and neo-Kantian literary theorist,[36] who means by it that the aesthetic experience does not propel us away from the aesthetic object but holds us in rapt attention. The aesthetic object, during the aesthetic experience, is the world. Symbolist and contextualist aesthetics are not identical, but there is a clear line of progressive development common to both. Though Yeats's theory is only asserted, whereas Vivas' is philosophically grounded, both endeavor to establish art as a uniquely valuable activity in man. In Yeats's words a work of art is neither an imitation of "objective" reality nor an adjunct of the poet's personality: ". . . the beryl stone was enchanted by our fathers that it might unfold the pictures in its heart, and not to mirror our own excited faces, or the boughs waving outside the window." [37] Taking the beryl stone as an emblem of the work of art, Yeats is suggesting that poetry is self-reflexive and that it generates its own world (the pictures in *its* heart).

Had he contented himself with these doctrines I think we could say fairly that Yeats was anticipating a contextual view of poetry. But, as the first generation of symbolists often did, he went beyond contextual boundaries (in the very same essay) because he felt the pressures upon him, partly of his own making, partly the making of his era, to find (in his own words) the "Sacred book," to elevate art not only to its own integrity, but also to seek in it the substitute for failing formal religion in a world of increasing secularity. These pressures, deeply subversive to a theory of poetic autonomy, led to such statements as this: Poets "make and unmake mankind, and even the world itself, for does not 'the eye altering alter all'?" [38] A theory of constructive perception has been carried to an unfortunate end. German idealistic philosophy—for the symbolists, the major source of their epistemology—begins to serve the vulgarizations of the poet who desires to make himself and (illogically) his fellow artists into solipsistic creators who through the imagination make a world that "has done with time." [39] Not satisfied with simply rejecting a naturalistic view of the artist as secretary by making him a magician, the symbolist tends to make him a priest and, finally, God the Father himself.

Disjunctive though they are, these two essays— "Symbolism in Painting," "The Symbolism of Poetry" —mark a high point in pure theory for Yeats. Though most of the critical writings of this early period are vitiated by inconsistency and incoherence, consistency and coherence in poetic theory are not the criteria by which the early Yeats should be judged. His dominant loyalties are no doubt symbolist *and* romantic; his singular trait at this time, however, was not an affiliation with any of the isms, but rather (as he suggested in his autobiographical aside) the constant questing and dis-

covering of places wherein he thought his problems
would be resolved. Symbolism was only one of those
places. "The Autumn of the Body" (1898) is a particularly fine example of the energetic confusion of his
thought. Beginning familiarly with an antinaturalistic
blast,[40] Yeats plumps for an aesthetic that will not
make art a handmaiden and for a "new poetry, which
is always contracting its limits." [41] But this more limited poetry is promptly expanded a few sentences later
when he again tries to make it an occultist slayer of
the naturalist dragon:

> Its [the new poetry's] importance is the greater
> because it comes to us at the moment when we
> are beginning to be interested in many things
> which positive science, the interpreter of exterior
> law, has always denied: communion of mind with
> mind in thought and without words, foreknowl-
> edge in dreams and in visions, and the coming
> among us of the dead, and of much else.[42]

And, he might have added later, interest in the transcendence of the aesthetic object; in the transference
of aesthetic value from the medium of its generation
and reference to an occult realm; in the creation, in so
many words, of a transcendental transparency that
forces the poet to look away from the world of time
and language. By the essay's end, Yeats has taken, because of his revulsion from the naturalistic view of
poetry, an apocalyptic stance which disregards all finite values:

> Man has wooed and won the world, and has
> fallen weary, and not, I think, for a time, but with
> a weariness that will not end until the last
> autumn, when the stars shall be blown away like
> withered leaves. He grew weary when he said,
> "These things that I touch and see are alone real,"
> for he saw them without illusion at last, and
> found them but air and dust and moisture.[43]

Assuming his role as magician, he seeks that "perfect
alembic" wherein all empirical experience will be ut-

54

terly dissolved, and in taking up those "burdens that have fallen from the shoulders of priests" [44] he has reunited aesthetic and transcendental values. Poetry has been vindicated once again, but the poet has left nature in search of the new home of the gods. [45]

All the confusion and complexity of Yeats's discussion of symbolism are fortunately held in check when he discusses two of his early passions, Shelley and Blake. [46] As much as Yeats was fascinated by Blake's theories of mind and reality, he succeeded surprisingly well in distancing himself from them, and his reservations imply a fundamental understanding of the basic theoretical weaknesses of romantic aesthetic and underscore his underlying acceptance of a naturalistic universe as well. A good example is his statement about Rossetti: "His poetry often wearies us as the unbroken green of July wearies us, for there is something in us, some bitterness because of the Fall, it may be, that takes a little from the sweetness of Eve's apple after the first mouthful. . . ." [47] Again and again in Yeats, what surprises is not the radical shifts in the development of his aesthetic, but the maturation and flowering of ideas casually dropped in his early career. The idea behind his phrase "vision of evil," elaborated in A Vision in 1925, had already appeared in the autobiographical writings published in 1922, and even earlier in the 1902 essay on Rossetti, "The Happiest of the Poets." Each time Yeats was noticing the lack of such a vision in romanticism. The idea implies the uneasy recognition that he was living, not in an idealistic, unfallen universe, but in a materialistic one.

In the essays on Shelley and Blake, Yeats pokes at the weakest points of romanticism with a sureness that actually makes his self-deprecating letter of 1903 (quoted at the beginning of this chapter) somewhat inaccurate. Like Stevens after him, he finally found romantic theory invalid, but the beauty of a myth of total resolution, of an imagination spiritually integrated with nature, was not easily put out of mind. He suggests, for example, the kinship of one of his favorite occulist doctrines, *Anima Mundi*, with Shelley's views, when he sees the *Anima* as continuous with the human imagination: ". . . Our little memories are but part of some great Memory that renews the world and men's thoughts age after age, and that our thoughts are not, as we suppose, the deep, but a little foam upon the deep. Shelley understood this. . . ." [48] Further on in the same essay Yeats seems about to take the easy way out of naturalism by accepting at face value the loosing of the poetic imagination from the restraints of time, place, and language: as the "poet of essences and pure ideas" he can "escape from the barrenness and shallowness of a too conscious arrangement." [49] Only his dogged self-honesty kept him from anachronistically repeating Shelley's performance. At the essay's conclusion Shelley is seen as the unconscious secretary to *Anima Mundi*, and as one "who hated life." [50] This criticism, drawn from Shelley's own explicit commitment to the visionary imagination in "A Defence of Poetry," implicitly rejects those idealistic views of poetry which, carried to their logical ends, strip the poet of any personal shaping powers and, finally, make personal shaping irrelevant. In romantic idealism a poem is not a thing whose being is achieved in and through language, but a confluence precluding language, at a visionary level, of the identity of the beautiful, the good, and the true with the perceiving mind.

The essays on Blake are the most interesting of all, for they dramatically realize Yeats's latent antiromanticism. If romantic theory, spiritualism, and the magical strain in the symbolist aesthetic tended to lift him out of time and beyond the pressures of an alien world, his skeptical mind tended to make him shy from a view of the poet and reality which ignored the mire of empirical experience and ignored the necessity of the artist's working within the limits of his chosen medium. In Yeats's emerging theory of poetry, the poetic

56

imagination needed grounding in a language that was neither an emanation from the One, nor the counter of empiricist epistemology. The complicated Blake-Yeats relationship has been carefully analyzed by Hazard Adams. Here I would stress the ambivalence of the Blake essays published in *Ideas of Good and Evil*, and first written in 1897. One of them, "William Blake and the Imagination," appears to accept Blake's version of romantic coherence without reservation.[51] The second essay, "William Blake and His Illustrations to the *Divine Comedy*," begins where the first left off—this time in an almost enchanted romantic posture—then pulls up short with a comment that knifes through the idealistic structure of romanticism:

> The limitation of his view was from the very intensity of his vision; he was a too literal realist of imagination, as others are of nature; and because he believed that the figures seen by the mind's eye, when exalted by inspiration, were "eternal existences," symbols of divine essences, he hated every grace of style that might obscure their lineaments.[52]

In one phrase—"he was a too literal realist of the imagination, as others are of nature"—Yeats put his finger on the inherent difficulties of both romanticism and naturalism. In both theories, craft and language have only secondary roles. Yeats's task is to write a poetry of the finite imagination immersed in human experience, yet not subject to the naturalistic reduction of poetic language. Concrete proposals for such a poetry were yet to come. For now he had left the task of sloughing off what he took to be the Blakean imagination and getting back into a world of action. The two antithetical views of the poet which Yeats wrestled with in his early career are perfectly counterpointed in this passage:

> [Blake] was very certain that he and Dante represented spiritual states which face one another in

an eternal enmity. Dante, because a great poet, was "inspired by the Holy Ghost"; but his inspiration was mingled with a certain philosophy, blown up out of his age, which Blake held for mortal and the enemy of immortal things, and which from the earliest times has sat in high places and ruled the world. This philosophy was the philosophy of soldiers, of men of the world, of priests busy with government, of all who, because of the absorption in active life, have been persuaded to judge and to punish, and partly also, he admitted, the philosophy of Christ, who in descending into the world had to take on the world; who, in being born of Mary, a symbol of the law in Blake's symbolic language, had to "take after his mother," and drive the money-changers out of the Temple. Opposed to this was another philosophy, not made by men of action, drudges of time and space, but by Christ when wrapped in the divine essence, and by artists and poets, who are taught by the nature of their craft to sympathise with all living things, and who, the more pure and fragrant is their lamp, pass the further from all limitations, to come at last to forget good and evil in an absorbing vision of the happy and the unhappy. The one philosophy was worldly, and established for the ordering of the body and the fallen will; . . . the other was divine, and established for the peace of the imagination and the unfallen will. . . .[53]

As early as 1897, just when his romantic and magical obsessions were strongest, Yeats was gesturing in the direction of a poetic that would reject the idealistic foundation of his nineteenth-century inheritance. The new poetic, rooted in the fallen world, would demand that the poet be a drudge of time and space; that he always sympathize with finite things; that he never forget the inextricable mixture of good and evil; that he write, in short, a poetry of the fallen will, a poetry immersed in a world of natural things behind which God or the One or spirit did not lurk. And it would not matter if God were indeed there, since the modern poet no longer possessed the penetrative vision of the unfallen poet. But most of all this fallen poet would love, not hate, "those graces of style"; in his naturalistic universe, language was all that he could ever be sure he had. Yeats said, in the letter quoted at the beginning of this chapter, that *Ideas of Good and Evil* was true, but no longer true for him. The reasons why are implicit in the very book he disavowed.

The conclusion to his flirtation with romantic theory appears in what may well be the most significant postscript in modern literature, written in 1924 for a new edition of his essays and appended to the second Blake essay:

> Some seven or eight years ago I asked my friend Mr. Ezra Pound to point out everything in the language of my poems that he thought an abstraction, and I learned from him how much further the movement against abstraction had gone than my generation had thought possible. Now, in reading these essays, I am ashamed when I come upon such words as "corporeal reason," "corporeal law," and think how I must have wasted the keenness of my youthful senses. I would like to believe that there was no help for it, that we were compelled to protect ourselves by such means against people and things we should never have heard of.[54]

The Pound-Yeats relationship is still uncharted, and, from a historical point of view, could remain so for a long time. A number of critics believe that Yeats was made a major poet because of his close contact with Pound in the second decade of this century. In a thorough review of the facts, Thomas Parkinson cogently suggests that such a contention cannot be proved and is gratuitous at any rate. Parkinson concludes too quickly, however, that a "sharp fundamental opposition of temperament and interests doomed them to ultimate disagreement," and, thus, "aesthetically" they steadily "grew apart." [55] The ideals of Pound's poetics, from his beginning with a static theory of the image to his final position which views the poet as neither romantic nor symbolist but as one who acts through his shaping will in history, are recognizable in the early Yeats who was often heading in a very similar direction. By later career there can be little doubt that for all meaningful considerations, the Yeatsian aesthetic was one that placed prime emphasis (1) on the poetry of existential immersion, and (2) on the importance of a finite, shaping will functioning freely in the particular poet at a particular time and place. The cosmic windows of romantic and symbolist aesthetic were blackened.

In the early days there was no way of avoiding abstractions because, as Yeats so rightfully pleads, he and his friends had to protect themselves from science—"people and things we should never have heard of." What *Ideas of Good and Evil* presents, in large measure, is what Yeats came to believe was an easy but dishonest way out: around the enemy and back to the claims of romanticism, or to those aspects of symbolism that sprung the poet, by means of a magical imagination, right out of time; back to those "fanatical hungry" faces of the spirtualists whose abracadabra would accomplish the same thing. But Yeats's awareness of a viable modern poetic can be detected even in *Ideas of Good and Evil;* this awareness in juxtaposition to his affair with nineteenth-century theories produces the incongruities that characterize most of the book. Among the essays that close *Ideas of Good and Evil,* *"The Return of Ulysses"* is a reflector of his clashing motivations. Yeats first identifies himself with the movement whose writers, he says, have a "lyrical and meditative mind" and delight "to speak with . . .

[their] own voice[s] and to see nature in the mirror of . . . [their] mind[s]." [56] The idea of a poem that reflects the particular dramatic experience of a particular artist does not fit with the other idea of a poet who, like "all the great mystics," becomes a "vessel of the creative power of God; and whether he be a great poet or a small poet, we can praise the poems, *which but seem to be his,* with the extremity of praise that we give this great ritual [of nature] which is but *copied* from the same eternal model" (italics mine). [57] The theory of the poet who shapes nature in his own kind of vision, and the theory of the poet who becomes instead a secretary to a supernatural artist—a poet, that is, without imaginative freedom—could not dominate simultaneously. Explicit and consistent realization of the way out was yet to come.

TOWARD A YEATSIAN POETIC OF WILL

The day before Yeats wrote the letter to John Quinn in which he expressed his displeasure with *Ideas of Good and Evil,* he wrote to George Russell and told him that the "close of the last century was full of a strange desire to get out of form, to get to some kind of disembodied beauty. . . . I feel about me and in me an impulse to create form, to carry the *realization* of beauty as far as possible" (italics mine). [58] The letter to Quinn said much the same thing: "I will express myself, so far as I express myself in criticism at all, by that sort of thought that leads straight to action, straight to some sort of craft." [59] I would like to say that 1903 was for Yeats a watershed year, but that would not be accurate because his thought could rarely be so neatly categorized as the metaphor demands. He would always be allured by those aspects of romantic and symbolist theories which promised imaginative penetration of a world beyond time. A more accurate generalization about his development

61

might run something like this: In the period when the essays of *Ideas of Good and Evil* were being written, Yeats's search for an adequate aesthetic was thrusting toward his nineteenth-century inheritance from romanticism and symbolism; after *Ideas of Good and Evil* the thrust was toward an aesthetic distinctly antipathetic to such purely idealistic or magical theories of poetry. His new theory—what I am calling the poetics of will and impersonality—is close to Stevens' theory of the finite imagination and is especially compatible with that existential and naturalistic view of reality which is the backdrop of much of modern literature.

The poetics of will is a poetics framed in tragic awareness; for Yeats, tragedy is precisely the naturalistic and existential fate that is forced upon the modern poet who is frank enough to admit that a cosmically framed aesthetic is not valid for him:

> As life goes on we discover that certain thoughts sustain us in defeat, or give us victory over ourselves or others, and it is these thoughts, tested by passion, that we call convictions. Among subjective men (in all those, that is, who must spin a web out of their own bowels) the victory is an intellectual daily recreation of all that exterior fate snatches away, and so that fate's antithesis. . . . We begin to live when we have conceived life as tragedy.[60]

The passage is extraordinarily rich and can, if we like, be explicated by the "system" so elaborately presented in *A Vision*. We need not refer to that system, however, to see the relevance of the passage to Yeats's newly emerging aesthetic. The image here of the subjective man—in Yeats, the imaginative man, the poet —spinning out poetry in a universe where creativity is theoretically denied, parallels Yeats's view of himself as a shaper, a maker of poems in a given linguistic medium, and in a world vacated by the gods of romanticism. The victory that Yeats achieves is similar to

Stevens' achievement of imaginative order: it is only momentary, too often illusory, always to be re-created daily. For the poet who conceives life as tragedy sees a reality without objective idealistic value, and he has no prophetic knowledge that his own values and orders mean very much in the long run. Poetry becomes more the various dramatic, depersonalized, and objectified gestures and postures of a man caught in a deterministic world of action than a grandiose breakthrough to a structure of reality envisioned by some of Yeats's predecessors. Poems are simply things a man makes, because he is a maker; they are not things apprehended in transcendent vision because the currents of ultimate being roll through him. The making of poetry is, finally, the fruit of the tragic victory, an assertion of freedom which a mechanistic universe will deny.

The new poetic demanded that Yeats resolve an apparent paradox. How can he involve himself in a finite universe (which he understands to be a necessary act) and still become a creative artist, rather than simply a secretary to this world of brute fact as Zola or Balzac would have it? How (as the Kantians would formulate it) can the imagination retain its freedom in a world of necessity? If the answer lies in the very making of poetry, and I have suggested it does, then *how* and *why*? As usual, Yeats's answers to complex questions are sometimes complex, sometimes tremendously naïve. He would assert, for example, though not argue very well, that Berkeley and Kant had proved that mind is epistemologically active and constitutive of the natural world. Sometimes he would feel so pressed on the issue of freedom that he would take the self-contradicting solipsistic view (usually an inherent danger of idealistic epistemology) which holds that everything is a representation of the self. In the last analysis, his interest in epistemology seems to me rarely to have been scholarly and disciplined, but, rather, pragmatic and expedient.[61] If you want to say

63

that the naturalists are wrong, and if you want to appeal to authority, then you appeal to Berkeley and Kant—at least as a starter. It is not surprising that Yeats, in his excitement to answer the tough questions posed by the tormentors of his youth—Darwin, Huxley, Tyndall, Marx—slipped into solipsism. But the truly significant responses to the challenges he faced were aesthetic, not philosophical, and aesthetic in the sense that his primary attention was to his artistic medium. To encompass his view of the self trapped in history, he elaborated an aesthetic of a freely creative and impersonal will.

Yeats's interest in a theory of impersonality appeared early and was probably gestated during his affair with the contextual implications of symbolist theory. But when he grew out of symbolism his view of impersonality changed, and what he finally meant by the term was not what Mallarmé meant, nor what the contextualists mean when they use the word. Impersonality in symbolist theory is the defining characteristic of the purely objective, autotelic poem. For the later Yeats the idea was not seen in these dimensions: it was a way of ensuring freedom and a way of saving creativity in a naturalistic universe. In the passage cited above, where the poet's tragic circumstances are outlined, Yeats went on to say that " 'the Mask' is an emotional antithesis to all that comes out of this [the poet's] internal nature." The end of the poetic process for Yeats is the creation of masks that are independent of the determined "Freudian" personal self, and free from the tyranny of personal emotion as well. The mask provides the release from necessity.

The theory of impersonality is first recorded by Yeats in his *Autobiography* as an expression of dissatisfaction with the manner of his early poetry. Yeats did not say there that personally felt emotion was undesirable but that it must be made "cold." [62] He addressed himself a number of times to the problem of impersonality in the *Autobiography,* and some of the more fertile passages suggest that impersonality (besides being the "antithesis of personal action and desire," an "achievement of an anti-self, a mask that delineates a being in all things the opposite to . . . [the poet's] natural state," and an escape from the "hot-faced bargainers and money-changers") is most basically *a mode of poetic imagery "always opposite to the natural self or the natural world"* (italics mine).[63] Together these aspects of impersonality contribute to a theory of poetry which meets Yeats's diverse requirements. To the utilitarians who demanded that a poem be good for something, and to the naturalists who asked that the poet ground himself only in empiricist epistemology and imitative poetics, the mask (as an impersonal, linguistic construct) was an answer. For his philosophy of the self caught in its own private actions, the idea of impersonality was a necessary corollary: "Does not all art come when a nature, that never ceases to judge itself, exhausts personal emotion in action or desire so completely that something impersonal, something that has nothing to do with action or desire, suddenly starts into its place?"[64] In the impersonal mode direct, or personal, emotion is abstracted from the natural self, and that natural self is in turn abstracted—it becomes an antiself—when it is lifted out of the natural world. This process of abstraction does not mean that Yeats sought an abstract art in the sense of Picasso's art of nonorganic forms, but that he understood creation to be the very act of placing the personal and the natural in the medium of language where during the process of composition, the process of cold, precise modification and shaping, something different emerged.

Because of the creative role given to language in this view of poetry, the poem achieved is not subject to the transparency of naturalism or the higher transparency of romanticism; the poetic faculty is grounded in language. This all comes very close to the symbolist and contextualist claim that a poem so conceived has being; free from owing its value to a world of objects or an idealistic world of spirit, or the personality of the poet, its value is generated in and contained by language. I believe Yeats would agree with one important reservation: the poem, he would insist, and language, are adjuncts of a particular will (though not expressions of it) and as such do not have the independent status that a tree or a dog or a person has. Absolute organicism—and this is what some symbolist and contextualist doctrine calls for—is the trait of poems that live and grow without the guidance of a conscious creator.[65] For Yeats, the poetic puppet of romantic and naturalistic theory has become the puppeteer. The puppeteer, not the puppet, has freedom, and freedom is what Yeats was searching for when he searched for a poetic outside romanticism or naturalism. The theory that a feeling, empirical ego can be abstracted by an artistic ego which then makes masks and antithetical selves in language, is an insight beyond the compass of Schelling's or Locke's epistemology, and beyond the ken of the explicit determinism of some heavy-handed Freudian interpretations (in which the artist is doomed to regurgitate only the suppressed drives of his id through a process that is essentially an elaboration of dream).

Considered only in the realm of philosophical aesthetics, the notion of impersonality can get fairly elusive. Fortunately we have more than the disjointed comments in the *Autobiography* to rely on. After the turn of the century Yeats did a considerable amount of writing on the drama, much of it in a little magazine called *Samhain,* and much of that was related to his broader theoretical concerns. The poetics of impersonal will and the philosophy of a self engulfed by naturalistic experience now dominate, just as romantic and symbolist theory and spiritualism dominate the earlier writings. These essays contribute especially to our understanding of the nature of a poem conceived in relation to person. In the 1902 issue of *Samhain* Yeats introduces his theory of a drama of abstraction —a nonnaturalistic drama—as a casual comment on a performance of *Deirdre* he had recently seen:

It was the first performance I had seen since I understood these things in which the actors kept still enough to give poetical writing its full effect upon the stage. I had imagined such acting, though I had not seen it, and had once asked a dramatic company to let me rehearse them in barrels that they might forget gesture and have their minds free to think of speech for a while. The barrels, I thought, might be on castors, so that I could shove them about with a pole when the action required.[66]

Then, recalling a Sarah Bernhardt performance, he made the theoretical point: "The whole scene had the nobility of Greek sculpture, and an extraordinary reality and intensity. It made me understand, *in a new way*, that saying of Goethe's . . . 'Art is art because it is not nature'" (italics mine).[67] This new understanding of Goethe's aphorism, coupled with Yeats's interest in a nonnaturalistic drama, puts the work of *Ideas of Good and Evil* in proper perspective and illuminates the directions of his aesthetic views. In the context of his romantic and symbolist obsessions of the 1890's, art was art because it was out of time and nature, literally beyond, literally penetrative of a supernatural realm. Now nature and art are distinct (the naturalists lose again), not because of transcendence, since art remains in time, but because poetry achieves its primary existence in language purposefully shaped toward its own inner reality, rather than toward a reality outside itself. Focusing on dramatized voice and stylized acting, Yeats sought "an extraordinary reality" whose generation and full expression would be independent of the natural world as well as of the supernatural. Nineteenth-century transparency of an empirical or super-empirical kind could no longer compromise the freedom of the poetic faculty. Creation becomes a function of a particular will alone, and it is in this sense that "literature is always personal." [68] Again Yeats remains outside the pure impersonality of contextualism. The qualification is important because it underlines his view of the poet working within his particular vision.

The poetics of freely creative will and impersonality appears contradictory to the philosophy of the naturalistically immersed self, but is actually its fulfillment. Yeats believed that a great literature was still to be achieved in his era because the "newspapers, all kinds of second-rate books, the preoccupation of men with all kinds of practical changes, have driven the living imagination out of the world." [69] The implication that the "living imagination," the source of great literature, must be immersed in the world is a clear enough rejection of his earlier aesthetic theories: "Great as Shelley is, those theories . . . which he has built up . . . hurry him from life continually." [70] Yeats detailed further the mode of operation of a time-bound imagination in his description of the abstracted (or impersonal) aesthetic object. In the 1904 issue of *Samhain* he said: ". . . we have but contemplated life. . . . The subject of all art is passion, and a passion can only be contemplated when separated by itself, purified of all but itself." [71] The passion contemplated is not the passion disembodied, but the passion realized formally; abstracted by language, the passion is lifted out of the context of natural experience. The work of the Ibsen school, on the contrary, aims at a representation of the flux itself.[72] As far as Yeats was concerned this ideal was not only worthless but impossible to achieve: "If you copy Nature's moderation of colour you do not imitate her, for you have only white paint and she has light." [73]

The paradox of the will immersed in history, yet free

68

to create, is paralleled by the paradox of the aesthetic object that gives insight into naturalistic reality without being an imitation of it: "If you wish to represent character or passion upon the stage, as it is known to the friends, let us say, of your principal persons, you must be excessive, extravagant, fantastic even, in expression." [74] This is the artist talking now, not the occultist, and he is saying that artistic achievement for the poet lies in the conscious "distortion" of nature performed by language. As the years went on, Yeats would continue to speak more and more of the problems of expression and less and less of the problems of idealistic metaphysics: "Call it art for art's sake if you will," [75] he concluded in the 1905 issue of *Samhain*. He knew that unless the poem was understood and conceived primarily as a linguistic affair, its insight into the "preposterous pig of a world" would not be very penetrating. Early in April, 1904, in a letter to Russell, Yeats repudiated the last-chance romanticism of his play *Land of Heart's Desire*, where the theme of leaving the world of action and conflict was strong. He repudiated it because he found it essentially "false." The letter concludes with a brilliant and concentrated metaphor of his new poetic: "We possess nothing but the will and we must never let the children of vague desires breathe upon it nor the waters of sentiment rust the terrible mirror of its blade." [76] Not the mirror versus the blade, but the "mirror *of* its blade." Yeats's phrase at once amalgamates and resolves the seemingly paradoxical halves of his poetic. The carving blade implies the free and autonomous craftsman; the "terrible mirror" ties him to the world of necessity.

During the period 1903–1915, Yeats published a number of critical essays which are essential to our understanding of his emerging poetic of will. He wrote in the preface to his newly collected essays that he was concerned mostly with the art of drama, and the collection is appropriately entitled *The Cutting of an Agate* (1915). Implicit and explicit in much of this writing is not only the idea of the artist as a cutter of the stones of experience, but also a drive toward an impersonal mode of expression. The carving will became the instrument that transformed experience by abstracting it in language. Poetry began after action ceased: the mask or antiself was the end of the poetic process and a symbol of the free imagination working within a deterministic universe. The romantic or magical imagination is displaced.

The double theme of immersed self and impersonal artistry received its fullest treatment in "Discoveries" (1906), "Poetry and Tradition" (1907), and the capstone of the new collection, "Certain Noble Plays of Japan" (1916). Earlier, in a preface to Synge's *The Well of the Saints*, published in 1905, Yeats hinted at the new movement of his aesthetic theory when he made this comment on *The Secret Rose*: ". . . I had finished *The Secret Rose*, and felt how it had separated my imagination from life. . . ." [77] And in "Art and Ideas" (1913) he suggested that the flower of his new aesthetic was planted back in his days with the Cheshire Cheese group: ". . . I filled my imagination with the popular beliefs of Ireland, gathering them up among forgotten novelists in the British Museum or in Sligo cottages. I sought some symbolic language reaching far into the past and associated with familiar names and conspicuous hills. . . ." [78] While he was absorbing Irish folk tradition, and even reminding himself that his first obligation was to Ireland, Yeats was still playing with a poetic that, in its transcendental and idealistic persuasions, was a contradiction of any temporalizing and localizing of poetry. Something had to yield, and it was the transcendental imagination that gave way: ". . . there are moments when I cannot believe in the reality of imaginations that are not inset with the minute life of long familiar things and symbols and places." [79] These moments recurred with increasing frequency as Yeats grew older until he became certain that a "man should find his Holy Land where he first crept upon the floor." [80] The poet thus envisioned is not a saint or a mystic who is content to seek the center in God where all is "still and fixed," but one who is contented only by that which is "for ever passing away." [81] Poetry's source is the immersed self, the "struggle of the individual and the world." [82]

The other theme of Yeats's poetic, that of impersonality, has been the most difficult to define because the word is used in more than one sense (three by my count) while only one meaning is germane to his own thought. I have already indicated that his impersonality is a relative idea and not the absolute theory postulated by Mallarmé. "Impersonality" occurs pejoratively in Yeats when he talks about science and its influence on language: "One must not forget that the death of language, the substitution of phrases as nearly impersonal as algebra for words and rhythms varying from man to man, is but a part of the tyranny of impersonal things." [83] Another pejorative usage occurs in a discussion of the symbolist movement with particular reference, apparently, to Mallarmé's comparison of poetry to music: "In literature . . . we have lost in personality . . . but have found a new delight . . . in pure imagination, in all that comes to us most easily in elaborate music." [84] But, believing that language cannot be emptied of all human reference, Yeats added: "Music is the most impersonal of things, and words the most personal, and that is why musicians do not like words." [85] Later, in the same essay, he discusses his early interest in symbolist impersonality and his subsequent rejection of it.[86] For once those eternal enemies, the symbolists and the scientists, seem to be in the same camp. The scientific ideal is to make language wholly denotative and referential; abstract mathematics is a good illustration of the ideal achieved. The symbolist ideal, contrarily, is also to construct a special language, this time wholly nonreferential in both its "realistic" and psychological content. A Mallarméan poem should have, in theory, no reference to the poet's psychology and no reference to the external world: hence the requirement of a "pure" imagination, which, through its constructive operation, creates a self-sufficient poem. But Yeats, who has only the will left, as he said to George Russell, cannot possibly escape personality in this sense. His version of the relationship of self and reality, unbuttressed as it is by the universalizing idealistic conceptions of mind and reality, postulates a radically personal vision. The conclusion, however, that such a vision necessitates the expressive poetry of romanticism is erroneous because it forgets what Yeats saw as the primary task of the artist: to create impersonally, to make masks.

In "Poetry and Tradition" and in "Certain Noble Plays of Japan" Yeats clarifies and expands the meaning of the theory of impersonality by counterpointing it with his old object of hatred, deterministic naturalism. In these essays achievement in craft and technique carries a philosophical burden: the shaping power of the artist, his ability to make a style, becomes his decisive weapon against a poetics of imitation. Beginning with an attack on the moralism of the Victorian utilitarians—"They prefer the stalk to the flower, and believe that painting and poetry exist that there may be instruction . . ." [87]—Yeats moves easily into a position where impersonal will and freedom counter utility and determinism: "They complain much of that commandment that we can do almost what we will, if we do it gaily, and think that freedom is but a trifling with the world." [88] By doing what he wills, through calculated creation, the artist achieves both freedom and style: "In life courtesy and self-possession, and in the arts style, are the sensible impressions of the free mind, for both arise out of a deliberate shaping of all things. . . . Who should be free if he [the artist] were not?" [89]

Style, then, lifts the poet out of the necessary confrontation of self and fallen world which establishes the tragic situation; style is the victory over the tragic, that glitter in the eye described in "Lapis Lazuli":

> It is in the arrangement of events as in the words, and in that touch of extravagance, of irony, of surprise, which is set there after the desire of logic has been satisfied and all that is merely necessary established, and that leaves one, not in the circling necessity, but caught up into the freedom of self-delight: it is, as it were, the foam upon the cup, the long pheasant's feather on the horse's head, the spread peacock over the pasty. . . . This joy . . . always making and mastering . . .[90]

Years later, in an essay called "The Irrational Element in Poetry," Wallace Stevens would come to a similar conclusion. The parallel is striking. Their very definition of creativity is the willful escape through craft from subjective and objective determinism, the going beyond everything that can be predicted, beyond that "circling necessity." And that moment of the making of poetry—that "shaping joy,"[91] or the "gaiety of language," as Stevens put it—launches the self into a world of freedom. All this comes to the great writer with the achievement of impersonality as he withdraws "his thought out of his life that he may learn his craft."[92]

The culminating critical essay of this period, "Certain Noble Plays of Japan," summarizes the nature and value of the freely and abstractly created aesthetic object. The key is in the meaning of "Noh" itself, which is "accomplishment."[93] Again and again Yeats makes the point that value in art is achieved not through naturalistic approaches, but in deliberate abstract creation which he defines as the leaving out of "some element of reality as in Byzantine painting."[94] Careful not to go to the lengths of analytic cubism (which he rejects

73

quite decisively in a letter to his father [95]), his purpose is, paradoxically, to reach "some more powerful life" through "distance from life" and "elaborate words." [96] And this creation of a reality in language can be achieved, Yeats said, by locking out the "pushing world" outside through the various forms and techniques of the medium itself: "Verse, ritual, music, and dance in association with action . . . gesture, costume, facial expression," and, particularly in the Noh drama, through the marionette-like movements of stylized acting. [97] The value of an aesthetic object thus envisioned is in the release it provides from the "disordered passion of nature." [98] In Stevens the imagination has similar psychological value: by creating its own world in metaphor it neutralizes the "violence from without."

In a diary kept in 1909, and reprinted in part in the *Autobiography*, there are some passages that epitomize the intent of Yeats's aesthetic of creative will and impersonality. Freedom, style, and impersonality are the necessary trinity that absolves him from the scientific universe of "logic" and the "machine": [99] "I think that all happiness depends on the energy to assume the mask of some other self; that all joyous or creative life is a re-birth as something not oneself, something which has no memory and is created in a moment and perpetually renewed." [100]

SOME LATER RESTATEMENTS

From about 1916 or 1917, when the great poetry began to pour out, Yeats's critical prose lessened in significance with the notable exception of *A Vision*, which occupied him for a long time through two different editions. *A Vision*, together with *Per Amica Silentia Lunae*, has received about as much time and energy from scholars as the poetry. Both documents have been scrutinized with great patience and an immense fund of background knowledge in areas far outside poetry and aesthetics. What I do here with *Per Amica* and *A Vision* is to place them within Yeats's aesthetic thinking. What I find in *Per Amica* is not so much an escape into *Anima Mundi*, which would mean a return to the romantic aesthetic Yeats had already rejected, as a sorrowful understanding that, however much escape might be desirable, it is for all meaningful aesthetic considerations not possible. And, in *A Vision*, I find not a myth of resolution, but a myth of irresolution, an antimyth, so to speak, which accounts better for conflict, tension, immersion, and process than it does for a release from time.

Per Amica (1917) is in two parts. The first, "Anima Hominis," considers the mask and the poetics of impersonality; the second, "Anima Mundi," focuses on the philosophy of withdrawal from time against the philosophy of immersion in time. Viewed in the context of Yeats's developing aesthetic, *Per Amica* presents no problems; by itself it is a misleading document. The best way I have found to avoid misplacing its emphasis is to read the second part first, but even this approach leaves questions unanswered: How important, for example, is all the discussion of Neoplatonism and the "Great Memory"? Given Anima Mundi, what is Yeats's attitude toward it? Does Anima Mundi play a necessary role in the functioning of the poetic imagination? The "Anima Mundi" section of *Per Amica* begins with what appears to be the prelude to a rejection of the philosophy of involved will, and an exaltation of what is essentially timeless vision:

> You have discovered how if you can but suspend will and intellect, to bring up from the "subconscious" anything you already possess a fragment of. Those who follow the old rule keep their bodies still and their minds awake and clear, dreading especially any confusion between the images of the mind and the objects of sense.[101]

This suspension of will and intellect allows the poet freedom from the world of action through the old way, through transcendence of action and time rather than through the aesthetic of impersonality. It is the way of the saint and the mystic to the still and the fixed, not the way of the poet who must struggle in the flux, as Yeats said in "Discoveries" in 1906. The saint, though free from the world of action, is still the slave of God. Yeats would rather be free than canonized:

> There are two realities, the terrestrial and the condition of fire. All power is from the terrestrial condition, for there all opposites meet, *and there only* is the extreme of choice possible, full freedom. *And there the heterogeneous is, and evil, for evil is the strain one upon another of opposites;* but in the condition of fire is all music and all rest [italics mine].[102]

The lure of transcendence was always tempting, but honesty forced Yeats to accept a finite world which, though a prison, was the stuff of poetry: "The soul cannot have much knowledge till it has shaken off the habit of time and of place, but till that hour it must fix its attention upon what is near, thinking of objects one after another as we run the eye or the finger over them." [103] "Shelley," Yeats concludes, "calls our minds 'mirrors of fire,'" which is a way of saying that the romantic imagination is not free because it is tied to a function of reflecting the timeless. But, he added, "I . . . ask the question all have asked, 'what or who has cracked the mirror?' I begin to study the only self that I can know, myself." [104] *Per Amica* ends with Yeats fearing that Anima Mundi will make him a puppet rather than a freely acting shaper of language.[105] His final position in the essay is perhaps the most delicate (and curious) issue in his thought. Anima Mundi is not thrown away by any means (it seems to be part of his belief), yet in a crucial way belief becomes unimportant for the making of poetry. Yeats was no systematic thinker, so we waste time if we try to solve the problem that way. Anima Mundi is given no necessary role in Yeats's aesthetic of immersed self and impersonality, and I suspect that the reason is a fear of compromising his artistic autonomy.

The whole question of the relationship of belief and poetry may be put in a different and somewhat simpler way. Yeats would argue in *A Vision* that poems must be written in the world of experience where the "antinomies cannot be solved." [106] From the god's-eye view, history is solved, the tangled lines of human experience are given preordained design. But the god's-eye view is accessible to the poet only in fleeting and rare moments. At all other moments, experience presents itself as a series of unresolved contradictions without transcendental synthesis; the world of belief, then, and the world in which poems are created seem not to be significantly related.

As a statement of the impersonality theory which enables the poet to achieve freedom within a naturalistic context, "Anima Hominis" is not nearly so full as the critical, autobiographical, and epistolary documents written prior to *Per Amica*. One particular passage, however, is as important as any earlier one:

> We can satisfy in life a few of our passions and each passion but a little. . . . The passions, when we know that they cannot find fulfilment, become vision; and a vision, whether we wake or sleep, prolongs its power by rhythm and pattern, the wheel where the world is butterfly. We need no protection, but *it* does, for if we become interested in ourselves, in our lives, we pass out of vision [italics mine].[107]

Yeats is suggesting that the very life of poetry depends on breaking the naturalistic hold through depersonalization. Properly seen, the poetic process itself is an impersonal process and a free process. In Yeats, "free" means "creative."

77

Placed in the long line of works produced after *Ideas of Good and Evil,* the controlling ideas of *A Vision* (1925; 1938) are not new. This fact is obscured, however, by the elaborate analysis of the course of history and the human personality, the weird jargon, the geometry of wheels and intersecting cones and gyres, and those opaque tables of codification. Beneath it all there is, fortunately, a strong thematic thread, firmly drawn through the book, telling us almost all we need to know as students of Yeats's aesthetics: that the relationship of self and reality is not resolved in myths of coherence; that in a finite world the human condition is defined by doubt and (Yeats's favorite term) the antinomy: "Life is no series of emanations from divine reason such as the Cabalists imagine, but an irrational bitterness, no orderly descent from level to level, no water fall but a whirlpool, a gyre." [108] Caught thus in history that is not "redeemed," as Eliot might have put it, the trapped self is, paradoxically, not less but more free. Not being an extension of higher, spiritual reality—in the sense of the continuity envisioned in romantic theory—being in fact totally cut off from divinity, man's freedom is absolute (a point that existentialist philosophy insists upon). This view, which I have been calling the philosophy of immersion and tension, is postulated by Yeats in a number of ways, and becomes a recurrent theme in *A Vision:*

1) My instructors used this single cone or vortex once or twice but soon changed it for a double cone or vortex, preferring to consider subjectivity and objectivity as intersecting states struggling one against the other.
2) Human life is impossible without strife.
3) Without this continual Discord through Deception there would be no conscience, no activity.
4) He [Shelley] lacked the Vision of Evil, could not conceive the world as continual conflict, so,

78

though great poet he certainly was, he was not of the greatest kind.

5) The whole System is founded upon the belief that the ultimate reality . . . falls in human consciousness . . . into a series of antinomies.

6) My instructors identify consciousness with conflict.

7) Neither between death and birth nor between birth and death can the soul find more than momentary happiness.[109]

"Antimony" generates *A Vision;* the idea of being caught in between is the source of all bitterness and conflict. In one of the truly revealing and lucid passages in the book, Yeats takes Paul Valéry to task for resolving in *Le Cimetière Marin* what he believed to be "unresolved antinomies": [110] ". . . after certain poignant stanzas and just when I am deeply moved he chills me. . . . And in a passage of great eloquence rejoices that human life must pass. I was about to put his poem among my sacred books, but I cannot now, for I do not believe him." [111] Whereas Shelley went up and out of time and evil, Valéry went down and into time and evil. Both resolved the antinomy because both dissolved a world. Yeats's quarrel with them was not literary at all, but philosophical. First, that irresolution, dualism, and evil are the facts of life does not mean that one happily embraces them. And honesty demands, he thinks, that one acknowledge the antithesis of dualism—monism, unity, resolution—as equally alluring and powerful principles, and vice versa. The exaltation of one over the other leads, finally, to an attenuation of poetic vision and a distortion of the way things are. In the full, ironic vision, the poetry of stasis (*Prometheus Unbound*) and the poetry of flux (*Le Cimetière Marin*) are perilously balanced.

Per Amica Silentia Lunae and *A Vision* together compose the last significant and direct attack on the core problems raised by Yeats's theoretical obsessions.

Though from 1925 on Yeats wrote a number of essays, only a few of them contain material vitally relevant to the enduring questions he had encountered in the 1890's. In the fertile period between the publication of *Ideas of Good and Evil* in 1903 and the first edition of *A Vision* in 1925, Yeats found that he had to get along without his inheritance from either Coleridge or Mallarmé. Among the later writings, those containing material reflective of the Yeatsian aesthetic are "Pages from a Diary Written in Nineteen Hundred and Thirty" (published posthumously in 1944) and the pieces recently collected in *Essays and Introductions:* "Bishop Berkeley" (1931), "Louis Lambert" (1934), "The Holy Mountain" (1934), "Modern Poetry: A Broadcast" (1936), and "A General Introduction for My Work" (1937). A few entries from the 1930 diary record the deeply ingrained antinomic vision: "If reality is timeless and spaceless that is a goal, an Ultimate Good. But if I believe that it is also a congeries of autonomous selves I cannot believe in one ever-victorious Providence." [112] The key word, of course, is *also*. Likewise, and closer to Yeats's poetic theory, freedom is understood as a function of the poetic imagination which feeds and operates within a context of necessity: "History is necessity until it takes fire in someone's head and becomes freedom or virtue." [113]

The view of idealistic epistemology in Yeats's essay on Berkeley is far more responsible than the one he had tried to convince T. Sturge Moore of five years earlier. When Yeats argued with Moore he pushed for complete license in solipsism. Anything that the mind conjured up was real; nothing existed outside our perception of it. Moore's replies were devastating; Yeats was hardheaded. But perhaps Moore had a salutary influence on him after all because he revised his position so that it became clearly compatible with his double commitment to the particulars of history and to poetry: "When I speak of idealist philosophy I think more of Kant than of Berkeley, who was idealist and realist alike, more of Hegel and his successors than of Kant. . . ."[114] Yeats's comments on Balzac speak to a similar point: ". . . whenever I have been tempted to go to Japan, China, or India for my philosophy, Balzac has brought me back, reminded me of my preoccupation with national, social, personal problems, convinced me that I cannot escape from our *Comédie humaine*."[115] When we consider the extreme antinaturalism that Yeats tended toward in early career and his lifelong flirtation with a romantic aesthetic, we have to admit that he has come a long way. Balzac's sense of particularity, his immersion in French history, are not now anathema but part of the necessary poetic.[116] And encompassing Yeats's Balzacian involvement is his poetic of impersonality, never better put than in his broadcast of 1936:

> A poet writes always of his personal life, in his finest work out of its tragedy, whatever it be; . . . he never speaks directly as to someone at the breakfast table, there is always a phantasmagoria. . . . he is never the bundle of accidents and incoherence that sits down to breakfast; he has been reborn as an idea, something intended, complete.[117]

Released from external determinism, yet still a mirror of sorts, the poet is also released from the determinism of the subjective ("all that is personal soon rots"[118]); his commitment to art (the "blade"), and his commitment to reality (the "mirror") are thus simultaneously met.

EPILOGUE: FICTIONAL BRIDGES TO POETRY

Of all Yeats's work, his short fiction has been most consistently neglected. An examination of this fiction as fiction is outside my scope, and, I would think, outside the limits of useful criticism. But Yeats's fiction is important because it gives us a dramatic sense of what the antinomies meant to him; an insight, too, into his never requited desire (despite his poetics of will) to get out of time, to dissolve the antinomies; and a sense of his equally strong motivations to live fully within the limits of finitude, to curtail all transcendental quests and be a man of action. The short stories, then, cannot be handled as discursive prose, or as if they were essays on the theory of poetry. They do, like so many of the poems, center on questions of the poet's value and power, but like the poems, too, they are imaginative renderings of the contradictions of experience, not doctrinal tracts. In these fictional bridges to the poems we get much more than the rational apologist for poetry: we get an image of the whole Yeats, the man of feeling as well as the man of thought.

In a little-known story called "Dhoya," published in book form in 1891 but finished, apparently, as early as 1887,[119] a man epitomizing physical strength (the title character) is inexplicably left alone on a deserted island. He is visited by a beautiful woman who, it turns out, is a faery from the otherworld. She soon falls in love with him, and her motivation is explained thus:

> "Dhoya, I have left my world far off. My people —on the floor of the lake are dancing and singing, and on the islands of the lake; always happy, always young, always without change. I have left them for thee, Dhoya, for they cannot love. Only the changing, and moody, and angry, and weary can love. I am beautiful; love me, Dhoya. Do you hear me? I left the places where they dance, Dhoya, for thee!" [120]

This woman's attraction to Dhoya, the attraction of stasis to change, is then turned about when Dhoya, in accepting her love, symbolically rejects that which defined his attractiveness: "He was very happy secluded in that deep forest. Hearing the faint murmurs of the western sea, they seemed to have out-lived change." [121]

Yeats further sketches in the ironic context in an authorial intrusion by suggesting a view of reality as nothing but process: "But Change is everywhere. . . . Every blood drop in their lips, every cloud in the sky, every leaf in the world changed a little. . . . All things change save only the fear of change." [122] The story ends when Dhoya commits suicide after losing his mate to one of the little folk in a game of chess. Permanence and change in this story are the terms of a painful antinomy, painful because Yeats's attitude is symbolized not by Dhoya alone, not by the woman, but by both. Together they represent the double attitude—simultaneous repulsion for and attraction to each term of his dualism.

Many of the stories and sketches printed in *The Celtic Twilight* (1893) are variations on a similar theme. A number of them present the need for change which the faery feels ("so peaceful that it was a little sad" [123]); others suggest the counterfeelings of the mortals who quest for stasis. A precise statement on the nature of the antinomic vision occurs in a context that implicitly rejects it:

It is one of the great troubles of life that we cannot have any unmixed emotions. There is always something in our sweetheart that we dislike. It is this entanglement of moods which makes us old, and puckers our brows and deepens the furrows about our eyes. If we could love and hate with as good heart as the Sidhe do, we might grow to be long-lived like them.[124]

On the whole, however, *The Celtic Twilight* is weighted by transcendental motivation. The concept of the poet implicit is that of prophetic seer, not maker, and he is symbolized by Raftery, the blind Irish balladmonger.[125] As the verse epilogue of the volume suggests that escape to the otherworld is desirable,[126] the antinomy is resolved in favor of a transcendent, rather than a finite, imagination.

In 1897 Yeats published two more volumes of stories which, taken together, shift his center of awareness back to the idea of the "Dhoya" story. The first, *The Secret Rose,* measures up pretty well to his own estimation in the preface to Synge's *The Well of the Saints* —his imagination was taken out of time. The tone, however, is a bit more complex than his assessment indicates. Five of the stories revolve about a figure who is associated with supernatural powers, and yet has sympathy with the Irish peasant, the natural. In "Out of the Rose" a heroic old knight defends some poor Irishmen from thieves, is wounded in the fight, and dies unattended and unburied. In "The Crucifixion of the Outcast" a Druid-like figure is stoned by beggars, and in "The Wisdom of the King" a benevolent leader who was "touched" as a child is alienated from his subjects when he learns of his strange past. The pattern seems an extension of *The Celtic Twilight,* and an implicit call to dissolve the antinomy by taking flight from the world of necessity.

In the other volume published in 1897, *Stories of Red Hanrahan,* Yeats suggests the antinomic vision again by sketching his title hero as a figure hung by his own divided experience. Red Hanrahan, "the great songmaker," is about to marry his sweetheart (in distress) Mary Lavelle, when he is irresistibly drawn into a card game with a weird old man. During the game the old man works his faery powers on Hanrahan and then leads him on a nightmarish chase. After a long, exhausting run Hanrahan finds himself alone beside a door on a barren mountaintop. He enters and steps (of course) into the realm of faery where he is offered supernatural powers. For reasons not explained, Hanrahan refuses the faery gifts and is promptly expelled. But to have been tempted was enough, and thereafter he is a visionary loner: Mary Lavelle is lost to another, his moments of transcendent insight are all too fleeting and rare, the Irish peasants regard him as an undesir-

able misfit. As a Yeatsian persona, Hanrahan symbolizes the poet caught between two worlds, neither of
which will have him.[127]

Perhaps the high point of Yeats's short fiction is the
strange occultist pieces in which Michael Robartes and
Owen Aherne make their first appearances: "Rosa Alchemica," "The Tables of the Law," and "The Adora-
tion of the Magi." The most important of the three for
Yeats's poetics, and particularly for his view of the
magical imagination, is the longest, "Rosa Alchemica,"
an account of a poet's semi-initiation into the mysteries
of an alchemical society. The intentional fusion of poetry and magic is explained as the artist's need for
transcendence through the reconstitution of an unsatisfactory reality:

> I had discovered, early in my researches, that
> their doctrine was no merely chemical fantasy,
> but a philosophy they had applied to the world,
> to the elements and to man himself; and that they
> sought to fashion gold out of common metals
> merely as a part of a universal transmutation of
> all things into some divine and imperishable sub-
> stance; and this enabled me to make my little
> book a fanciful reverie over the transmutation of
> life into art, and a cry of measureless desire for a
> world made wholly of essences.[128]

But the "cry" cannot be answered unless the poet becomes a full initiate, and that is doomed from the beginning when the narrator describes himself thus:
". . . in my most perfect moment I would be two
selves, the one watching with heavy eyes the other's
moment of content." [129] His sponsor, Michael Robartes, encourages him to cultivate his magical imagination because he is "miserable in the hustle and noise
of the multitude in this world and in time." [130] The
narrator's feelings are divided, however; when he con-
sents to go with Robartes and participate in the occult
rituals, he goes in "terror." [131] Upon arriving at the

temple of the Alchemical Rose, the narrator is ushered into a library, among whose books are Blake's prophetic writings. Not long after, and half unwilling, he is seen in the midst of "a magical dance" whose rhythm was the "wheel of eternity, on which alone the transient and the accidental could be broken and the spirit set free." Believing that he is losing the control of his will to some outside power, he pulls back from apocalyptic transmutation, faints, and breaks the spell.[132] The story ends with the narrator claiming that he is "half lost" to the supernatural, a dilemma similar to Red Hanrahan's. This summary of the action is probably sufficient to place "Rosa Alchemica" within the "Dhoya" pattern, but it does an injustice to the puppet symbolism that says so much about an important theoretical point.

In an essay of 1896 Yeats described the mystical poet (with some enthusiasm) as a "vessel of the creative power of God" whose poems "but seem to be his." But one year later, in "Rosa Alchemica," his latent fears about a supernaturally sanctioned aesthetic were suggested in his image of the magical poet as a puppet whose artistic will is controlled and directed by beings of a higher order. The transcendental promises of Robartes' philosophy, certainly attractive to Yeats, are overshadowed by the implicit compromise of artistic autonomy.

The magical imagination, like the secretarial imagination, implicitly postulates transparency and therefore a severe compromise of the artist's autonomy. I think we may go so far as to say that the quest for radical artistic freedom is the underlying continuity of Yeats's complex thought. For even in the 1890's, when his romantic and symbolist propensities were marked, it is clear from this description of Robartes what his reservations are: ". . . his sleeping face . . . was to my excited mind more like a mask than a face. The fancy possessed me that the man behind it had dis-

solved away like salt in water, and that it laughed and
sighed, appealed and denounced at the bidding of beings greater or lesser than man." [133] Likewise in this
description of himself: "I seemed to be a mask [not to
be confused with impersonality theory]. . . . Many
persons, with eyes so bright and still that I knew them
for more than human, came in and tried me on their
faces, but at last flung me in a corner laughing." [134]
The quest for a free imagination led Yeats into time
and a finite world, toward a theory of impersonality,
the mask of liberation, and away from the mask of
magic, the mask of imprisonment.

4

Implicit Poetics and the Transmutation of Doctrine: Contexts of Byzantium

> For one throb of the artery
> While on that old grey stone I sat
> Under the old wind-broken tree,
> I knew that One is animate,
> Mankind inanimate phantasy.
> "A Meditation in Time of War"

> Wine comes in at the mouth
> And love comes in at the eye;
> That's all we shall know for truth
> Before we grow old and die.
> I lift the glass to my mouth
> I look at you, and I sigh.
> "A Drinking Song"

YEATS is often read doctrinally as the prophet of various brands of philosophical idealism and occultism. Commenting on the first poem above, John Unterecker has written: "Reality is in the Platonic forms ('One is animate'); mankind is the shadowy imitation, the 'inanimate phantasy,' of the grand design."[1] But does Platonic doctrine adequately encompass Yeats's tone, or does it distort? Unterecker's summary and Yeats's poem are not the same thing, and the difference goes beyond rhythm and rime. The line "For one throb of the artery" is a strong qualifying preface to doctrine. What about all the rest of time? Is reality then in mankind, and are the Platonic forms merely a pleasant dream? What does Yeats believe before and after that brief moment? If we allow the poem to ask these questions, then what Yeats believes becomes very difficult to determine. Tone and attitude are not simple and pure, message is not so easy to extract.

Even if we allow the Platonic reading to stand by discounting the ironic possibilities, however, what are we to make of the second poem, by itself, and in relation to the first? Living bodily life as an end in itself, cherishing the sensual moment, is hardly what we expect of the Platonist. But "A Drinking Song" is not the response of a Platonist who intends to have his illusion and reality, too, for the sensual is (as far as we can know in this life) "all we shall know for truth," and not merely the prelude to a higher, an idealistic, truth. The two little lyrics balk at being brought together in a propositional synthesis.

In the pages that follow I am content to let stand what Yeats called his "unresolved antinomies." The idea is a pervasive one in his writings and lies at the very heart of his vision. Life presents itself to him as a series of dualisms, or contradictions, or antinomies. He might believe that history is ultimately redeemed, but he could rarely see it or experience it so. Trapped within the flux of time he could, at moments, intuit release from necessity and the innumerable afflictions dealt him in the everyday world. But for all his transcendental desires, Yeats often found life in the finite world attractive enough to lure him down from the occult towers, attractive enough, in fact, to make him wish he had never engaged in otherworldly pursuits: Yeats the man of action—lover, indomitable Irishman, politician—is no less "true" than Yeats the man of thought, the idealist who scorned the life of fish, flesh, and fowl. This chapter centers on the enormously suggestive and complex Byzantium poems which I think best express the tortuous dilemma of being caught in between clashing motivations: in the introductory section I assess the tone of the early poems through *Responsibilities* (1914) with the focus on Yeats's emerging dualistic vision; the conclusion is an analysis of "Lapis Lazuli"—*Last Poems* (1936–1939)—which I consider an ideal illustration of what I have called in chapter 3 the "poetics of will."

My point of view in this chapter is that poetry is not a bitter pill of doctrine which we swallow because it is sugared over with metaphors. Below I try to confine myself to the method of close verbal analysis which one doctrinalist claimed would produce a "superficial reading" [2] of Yeats. Perhaps, as Leslie Fiedler phrased it, what I am about to engage upon is an exercise in "higher remedial reading." Until we perform this exercise, however, I do not believe we have much ground to stand on when we say that Yeats fits here, there, or anywhere in the history of literature, philosophy, or religion.

VOYAGES TO BYZANTIUM: 1889–1914

In what we regard today as his first significant effort, "The Wanderings of Oisin" (1889), Yeats dramatizes the double-quest motif we first saw in the short story, "Dhoya." Too often we have taken Yeats's word on his early work as definitive. The much-quoted letter in which he says that his early poetry was "all a flight into faeryland from the real world, and a summons to that flight," [3] obscures the genuine doubt and vacillation, and sometimes deep irony, present in the early poems. The marriage of Oisin, the Celtic hero, and Niamh, the "unhuman" [4] goddess from the Celtic otherworld, exemplifes Yeats's mixed feelings. First of all, their marriage is not the amalgamation of permanence and change, but the transcendence of change. So far a familiar story for a fin-de-siècle poet: unable to live within a naturalistic universe he seeks to transcend it through the imagination. But, unlike one of the more traditional versions of the Oisin legend, Yeats's account intimates that all is not well in the timeless paradise. There, where "Time and Fate and Chance" are "mocked," and where neither "Change nor Death" can tyrannize, the otherworldly creatures are overcome by sadness at the mere mention of the human world Oisin has recently left.[5] And Oisin himself, though eager to wash from his cloak the "mire of a mortal shore," [6] without hesitation leaves the world of stasis to the immortals when he encounters a symbol of human time:

> When one day by the tide I stood,
> I found in that forgetfulness
> Of dreamy foam a staff of wood
> From some dead warrior's broken lance:
> I turned it in my hands; the stains
> Of war were on it, and I wept,
> Remembering how the Fenians stept
> Along the blood-bedabbled plains
> Equal to good or grievous chance:
> Thereon young Niamh softly came
> And caught my hands, but spoke no word
> Save only many times my name,
> In murmurs, like a frighted bird.
> We passed by woods, and lawns of clover,
> And found the horse and bridled him,
> For we knew well the old was over.[7]

Once back in time (he has been out of it for 300 years), Oisin sees his youth vanish; he becomes like Red Hanrahan, or several figures in a number of Yeats's later poems, "A creeping old man, full of sleep, with the spittle on his beard / never dry," [8] who yet possesses a painful vision of eternal youth: "Those merry couples dancing in tune, / And the white body

91

that lay by mine."[9] In this early poem, Yeats made a preliminary exploration of those symbols of sexual love, old age, and transcendence which face one another in ambivalent and antinomic opposition in some of the later poems.

In light of the double motivation implicit in "The Wanderings of Oisin," the most notable poem in Yeats's first collection, *Crossways* (1889), is "The Stolen Child," which plays on the Irish folk theme of the human child coveted by the faeries and whisked away by them to their world:

> *Come away, O human child!*
> *To the waters and the wild*
> *With a faery, hand in hand,*
> *For the world's more full of weeping than you*
>   *can understand.*[10]

Again, however, it is Yeats's modification of the traditional that distinguishes his particular vision. For all its undesirability, the world of weeping claims his affection; by dwelling on natural details he objectifies his ironic awareness:

> Away with us he's going,
> *The solemn-eyed:*
> He'll hear no more the lowing
> Of the calves on the warm hillside
> Or the kettle on the hob
> Sing peace into his breast,
> Or see the brown mice bob
> Round and round the oatmeal chest [italics
>   mine].[11]

But the ironic dimension achieved in "The Stolen Child" and "The Wanderings of Oisin" is exceptional in these early poems. More characteristically, thematic emphasis is placed solidly on retreat and unregretted transcendence of the natural world. Occasionally, though, the voice of the divided self comes through. In the companion pieces that begin the first volume, "The Song of the Happy Shepherd" and "The Sad Shep-

herd," the common theme is simultaneous lamentation
for the end of a romantic world and alienation from
the world newly defined by later nineteenth-century
science:

> The woods of Arcady are dead,
> And over is their antique joy;
> Of old the world on dreaming fed;
> Grey truth is now her painted toy;
> Yet still she turns her restless head:
> But O, sick children of the world,
> Of all the many changing things
> In the dreary dancing past us whirled,
> To the cracked tune that Chronos sings,
> Words alone are certain good.
>
> . . . .
>   Seek, then,
> No learning from the starry men,
> Who follow with the optic glass
> The whirling ways of stars that pass—
> Seek, then, for this is also sooth,
> No word of theirs. . . .[12]

In "The Sad Shepherd," the opponent of the scientific
enemy and the world of process is put to the test.
Finding nature inhumanly indifferent, the shepherd
decides to take his own advice:

> *. . . I will my heavy story tell*
> *Till my own words, re-echoing, shall send*
> *Their sadness through a hollow, pearly heart;*
> *And my own tale again for me shall sing,*
> *And my own whispering words be comforting,*
> *And lo! my ancient burden may depart.*
> Then he sang softly nigh the pearly rim:
> But the sad dweller by the sea-ways lone
> Changed all he sang to inarticulate moan
> Among her wildering whirls, forgetting him . . .[13]

Erected as a last defense against the ravages of science, narcissistic revery has failed the poet.

    Yeats's tone is not always so bleak. Though King

Goll has gone mad,[14] the implication in surrounding poems is that had he transcended the world of action instead of being engrossed in it, his story would have had a different ending. Thus, with the exceptions of "Fergus and the Druid" and "To the Rose upon the Rood of Time," the uncomfortable ironic perspective of "The Wanderings of Oisin" and "The Stolen Child" is lost, or, better, dissolved, just as the real world is dissolved by the alchemy of the magical imagination. Aware, apparently, that his transcending desires precluded his anchoring poetry in an alien, materialistic universe, and, particularly, in Irish political matter, Yeats concluded his second volume, *The Rose* (1893), with "To Ireland in the Coming Times," a piece that stands out because of its apologetic tone:

> *Know, that I would accounted be*
> *True brother of a company*
> *That sang, to sweeten Ireland's wrong,*
> *Ballad and story, rann and song;*
> *Nor be I any less of them,*
> *Because the red-rose-bordered hem*
> *Of her, whose history began*
> *Before God made the angelic clan,*
> *Trails all about the written page.*[15]

But you cannot "sweeten Ireland's wrong" by going to Innisfree. As an earlier draft of this poem makes abundantly clear, [16] the hideaway island, though not necessarily a symbol of the timeless, is certainly removed from the pressures of the real world, including those political in nature.

The author of "The Pity of Love," "The White Birds," and "A Faery Song" does not intend to go to Innisfree alone. Falling in love for the young Yeats signaled not the explicit commitment to the body (as it did for Donne), and thus an implicit commitment to the imperfection of natural things, but an even stronger reason for getting out of a threatening world:

> A pity beyond all telling
> Is hid in the heart of love:

The folk who are buying and selling,
The clouds on their journey above,
The cold wet winds ever blowing,
And the shadowy hazel grove
Where mouse-grey waters are flowing,
Threaten the head that I love.[17]

Similarly, in "The White Birds," the lover yearns for faeryland and a transformation of himself and his beloved into carefree supernatural birds:

I am haunted by numberless islands, and many a
  Danaan shore,
Where Time would surely forget us, and Sorrow
  come near us no more;
Soon far from the rose and the lily and fret of the
  flames would we be,
Were we only white birds, my beloved, buoyed
  out on the foam of the sea! [18]

And finally, in the first section of "The Man Who Dreamed of Faeryland," an island again becomes a metaphor for a supernatural world where lovers may retreat, unharried by the demands of time.

I suppose it is easy (and justifiable) to push aside many of these poems in Yeats's second volume as minor efforts at best. He is so far from creating in language a rich, many-sided reality which defies doctrinal interpretation that he has left himself wide open to didactic reduction. Perhaps, more lamentably, he has given us the emotionally shallow poetry of a love-struck boy. Usually it is as difficult to overrate the later Yeats as it is to underrate the earlier poet. This is old hat in Yeats criticism. But the old hat does not always fit; alongside these thin poems are others that betray the presence of a poet who can see much more than he is willing to admit. In "The Two Trees," for example, a dualistic vision of reality is evoked in two sections of equal length. One vision is of a fallen world where nothing is resolved; the other vision is of an Edenic world, corresponding roughly to the transcendent realm where all is harmony:

Beloved, gaze in thine own heart,
The holy tree is growing there;
From joy the holy branches start,
And all the trembling flowers they bear.
The changing colors of its fruit
Have dowered the stars with merry light. . . .

. . . .

Roots half hidden under snows,
Broken boughs and blackened leaves.
For all things turn to barrenness
In the dim glass the demons hold,
The glass of outer weariness,
Made when God slept in times of old.[19]

Though the poem ends with the admonition "Gaze no more in the bitter glass" that reflects a fallen world, the poet has in fact gazed there; what he has seen is not resolved in higher synthesis, and his dualistic vision stands.

"Fergus and the Druid," even more than "The Two Trees," describes an antinomy that tortuously hangs the poet between transcendence and acceptance of an imperfect universe. As he later became so fond of doing, Yeats here picks up a theme and a situation from an earlier poem and amplifies them. In this instance the earlier poem appears to be "The Madness of King Goll" which by itself presents a single view: the world of action has a malevolent influence on those men of political action who must wrestle with it. Now, in the sequel, Fergus gives his kingship to the more worldly Conchubar, lest he go mad: "So I laid the crown / Upon his head to cast away my sorrow." [20] When asked by a Druid what he needs to make him happy, Fergus answers: "Be no more a King, / But learn the dreaming wisdom that is yours." [21] But before the Druid gives him the "little bag of dreams," he warns Fergus as the stolen child, or Niamh, or the woman in "Dhoya" might have:

Look on my thin grey hair and hollow cheeks
And on these hands that may not lift a sword,

This body trembling like a wind-blown reed.
No woman's loved me, no man sought my help.[22]
Precisely those risks inherent in the realistic situation
are what Fergus wants to avoid and, conversely, what
the Druid needs to complete his experience. Unfortunately, it is only after Fergus is granted his wish that
he possesses the ironic knowledge that nothing can
totally suffice: "Ah! Druid, Druid, how great webs
of sorrow / Lay hidden in the small slate-coloured
thing!"[23] The realization that transcendence of the
human condition will not make all things right, that
there is trouble in paradise, places the otherworldly
poems in these early volumes in a less than definitive
perspective. Perhaps the best way to avoid placing too
much emphasis on the flight to faeryland is to see
Yeats's second volume, *The Rose,* through its opening
poem, "To the Rose upon the Rood of Time," wherein
the transcending imagination is invoked and then dis-
tanced with "Lest I no more hear common things that
crave."[24]

With the publication in 1899 of his third volume,
The Wind among the Reeds, Yeats appeared to be
making a last gesture toward unqualified transcendence. Poem after poem is the expression of an unini-
tiated Fergus who, unhappy with his worldly circumstances, can see nothing but release on the other side
of finitude. Given the fullness of his vision in, say,
"The Wanderings of Oisin" or "The Two Trees," the
performance of *The Wind among the Reeds* is an
attenuated one. Ironic awareness seems never to have
troubled Yeats, antinomic experience never to have
obsessed him. The theme of escape announced in the
first poem of the volume indicates, I believe, that the
struggle of self and world has been given up. No
solemn-eyed child looks back in sadness as "Niamh [is]
calling *Away, come away:/Empty your heart of its
mortal dream.*" The reason for heeding Niamh's call is
suggested in a poem not quite immediately following.
A lover, possessed by the extravagant feeling that the

97

whole world is "wronging" his woman's image, would like to transform the world:

> The wrong of unshapely things is a wrong too great to be told;
> I hunger to build them anew and sit on a great knoll apart,
> With the earth and the sky and the water, re-made . . .[25]

But it is not possible to remake reality, and willed transcendence appears to be the only answer: "Outworn heart, in a time out-worn, / Come clear of the nets of wrong and right."[26] The rest of the volume abounds with examples of the transcendence motif, sometimes expressed as simple escape, sometimes as the only way of requiting love, sometimes as the desire for violent destruction of the natural world by supernatural powers. And all the while frequent capital letters and vague images help to compose some of Yeats's worst lines.[27] Here, I believe his comment that his early work "was all confused, incoherent, inarticulate,"[28] is exactly to the point.

Between *The Wind among the Reeds* (1899) and *Responsibilities* (1914), Yeats drastically revised his aesthetic theory. The development was from romantic and symbolist theory to a philosophy of historical immersion and a poetic of impersonality. In the same period his poetic style underwent parallel development. Thomas Parkinson's two books on Yeats are detailed examinations of the emergence and fruition of his new style, and any comments I could make would merely repeat the substance of what Parkinson has said so well.[29] Thus, I shall restrict myself to the new theoretical emphasis implied, particularly in "Adam's Curse" (*In the Seven Woods,* 1904) and "The Dolls" (*Responsibilities*).

"Adam's Curse" is unlike anything that Yeats had yet written because it is substantially about the poetic process itself. The idea of the poem—that the making of a style is a difficult but prime requisite rendered all the more necessary by the "fallen" nature of the world: Adam's curse—had been expressed before (1897) in an essay on William Blake which marked an important transition in Yeats's theory of poetry. Toward the end of that essay, Yeats wrote a long comparison of Blake and Dante which amounted to a summary of the nature and weaknesses of the romantic imagination. Particularly, Yeats saw that a visionary conception of the creative process postulated a transparent poetic entity: the poetic medium, relegated to a mediative role, functioned as a window through which the reader could view what the poet had already seen in unmediated vision—the idealistic universe. In an idealistic universe perhaps the function of language can be no higher. But Yeats saw his universe naturalistically, and, with the romantic possibilities now gone, if he were to eschew the magical imagination of symbolism as well as the secretarial imagination of literary naturalism, both of which postulate transparent poetic entities, then the only things left are language itself and the power of artistic will to shape it. Craft becomes almost everything:

> A line will take us hours maybe;
> Yet if it does not seem a moment's thought,
> Our stitching and unstitching has been naught,
> Better go down upon your marrow-bones
> And scrub a kitchen pavement, or break stones
> Like an old pauper, in all kinds of weather;
> For to articulate sweet sounds together
> Is to work harder than all of these. . . .
>
> . . . .
> It's certain there is no fine thing
> Since Adam's fall but needs much labouring.[30]

The new theory of poetry rejects transcendence, but Yeats never forgot the exciting possibilities raised by his toying with romantic and symbolist theory. His intense Byzantium poems seem to indicate that his doctrine of impersonality, though it may have satisfied his purely theoretical side, could not pacify him emotionally. The great conflicts of the 1890's—art versus nature, time versus transcendence—continued to plague him. One of the last poems in *Responsibilities*, "The Dolls," is also one of the best of Yeats's earlier confrontations of a recurrent theme:

A doll in the doll-maker's house
Looks at the cradle and bawls:
"That is an insult to us."
But the oldest of all the dolls,
Who had seen, being kept for show,
Generations of his sort,
Out-screams the whole shelf: "Although
There's not a man can report
Evil of this place,
The man and the woman bring
Hither, to our disgrace,
A noisy and filthy thing." [31]

The image of the doll, an artifact, is opposed to the natural image of the baby, "'A noisy and filthy thing.'" Abstracting the images from the poem, the opposition of art and nature seems clear enough. But why, if the realms of art and nature are irreconcilable, do the dolls feel insulted (by sexuality?)? "The Dolls" is simply not subtle enough to embody the full possibilities. We need to turn to "Sailing to Byzantium," "Byzantium," and "Lapis Lazuli."

THE BYZANTIUM POEMS

Both Mr. [R. P.] Blackmur and Mr. [Cleanth] Brooks— Mr. Brooks more than Mr. Blackmur—show us the systematic implications of the symbols of the poem "Byzantium." The presence of the system at its most formidable cannot be denied to this poem. I should like to see, nevertheless, an analysis of it in which no special knowledge is used. I should like to see it examined with the ordinary critical equipment of the educated critic. . . . The symbols are "made good" in the poem. . . .

Allen Tate, "Yeats's Romanticism:
Notes and Suggestions"

> In abstract or geometrical art . . . we desire to create a
> certain . . . shape, which, being durable and permanent
> shall be a refuge from the flux and impermanence of out-
> side nature. The need which art satisfies here is not the
> delight in the forms of nature, which is a characteristic of
> all vital arts, but the exact contrary. . . . there is an at-
> tempt to purify . . . the messiness, the confusion, and the
> accidental details of existing things. . . . The necessary
> presupposition is the idea of disharmony or separation be-
> tween man and nature.
>
> T. E. Hulme, *Speculations*

"Sailing to Byzantium" and "Byzantium" are among the most fascinating and most difficult of all Yeats's later writings. There are more than fifty commentaries on the poems, including those in book-length studies of Yeats.[32] I find it surprising, given this amount of scholarship, how often the Byzantium poems are read as sheer doctrinal quests, or as bright statements of belief in a transcendental theory of art. Rarely are they considered on their own terms, as poems, as pieces of language that function differently from prose statement. It is my point that the two poems articulate a dark antinomic vision of reality, and that they are best read as self-contained contexts, rather than as illustrations of the Yeatsian system.[33]

The particular prose statement most critics have in mind when they think about the Byzantium poems occurs in *A Vision:*

> I think if I could be given a month of Antiquity
> and leave to spend it where I chose, I would
> spend it in Byzantium a little before Justinian
> opened St. Sophia and closed the academy of
> Plato. I think I could find in some little wine-shop
> some philosophical worker in mosaic who could
> answer all my questions, the supernatural de-
> scending nearer to him than to Plotinus even.
> . . . I think that in early Byzantium, maybe
> never before or since in recorded history, reli-
> gious, aesthetic and practical life were one. . . .[34]

Historical Byzantium becomes the symbolic good place for Yeats because there he would achieve "Unity of Being"; there the finite and the infinite merge. But since the historical city cannot be recovered, it becomes converted into a city of imagination: Byzantium is a state of resolution and stasis outside nature. Yeats's allusion to Byzantine art suggests the antithesis of organic versus abstract art. In art that offers the organic forms of nature as its norm, the artist feels beneficently located within the universe and creates in empathy with natural forms, which he holds are alive with spirit. The psychic presuppositions of abstract art are directly opposed to those of organic art. As the German aesthetician, Wilhelm Worringer,[35] has pointed out, the abstract artist employs geometric forms over organic forms and purposefully distorts and stylizes his images of reality because nature, regarded as the absurd, inhuman "other," is now apprehended with dread. The artist of the abstract seeks permanence and release from naturalistic process in the making and contemplation of art objects whose laws of creation disregard the natural world. Yeats, if he could, would like to be abstracted to the same permanence and release. This is the theoretical background of the poems, and a sketch of their progressions if we read them through the ideas explicit and implicit in the passage from *A Vision*.

> That is no country for old men. The young
> In one another's arms, birds in the trees
> —Those dying generations—at their song,
> The salmon-falls, the mackerel-crowded seas,
> Fish, flesh, or fowl, commend all summer long
> Whatever is begotten, born, and dies.
> Caught in that sensual music all neglect
> Monuments of unageing intellect.

The first stanza of "Sailing to Byzantium," as *A Vision* promises, is an indictment of the sensuality of animal life. Ostensibly it is not a statement of the tension between body and mind, but of the superiority of mind. The dwelling on sensuality indicates, however, that the speaker is not entirely above the wants of the body. "That country"—the images are sufficiently generalized to make it any country—is said to be undesirable for several reasons. From the wise perspective of an old man we are told that animal life is a rather messy affair ("mackerel-crowded seas"), a rather painful affair ("salmon-falls"), and a terribly futile experience ("Whatever is begotten, born, and dies"). But for an old man it is painful in a more special sense. The implication of the punning in line 3 ("dying generations") is that this old man's understanding of reality is framed in part by those ambiguities coalescing in the sexual act, which he can no longer perform. The young have been dying (literally) from the moment they were born, and they are "dying" in another way when "in one another's arms." The tone of lines 5-6 suggests that no one but he, the wise old man, knows that the sexual embrace is only a preface to permanent loss of self in physical death. That he actually feels this way seems to be suggested by the sardonic irony that makes animal life celebrate not only itself but its own end: "Fish, flesh, or fowl, commend all summer long / Whatever is begotten, born, and dies." The separation of the world of the body and the world of the mind is insisted upon in the concluding lines of the stanza: "Caught in that sensual music all neglect / Monuments of unageing intellect." By the old man's own logic, cultivation of the senses predicates neglect of the mind. Yet it is not all that impersonal: it is the monumental creations of his intellect, or those of other, dead artists, which are being neglected. In view of his evocation of natural life as sexually oriented, the young can have nothing to do with "cold" monuments of art, a strange characterization that becomes particularly meaningful if we understand a monument to be not only "living" art, but also a sepulchre of the dead, the antithesis of the living. The metaphor would imply the alienation of the artist from "that country." Caught in sexual "death," the young are not going to have much commerce with a ridiculous and sexually powerless old man, the mortal maker of art works.

> An aged man is but a paltry thing,
> A tattered coat upon a stick, unless
> Soul clap its hands and sing, and louder sing
> For every tatter in its mortal dress,
> Nor is there singing school but studying
> Monuments of its own magnificence;
> And therefore I have sailed the seas and come
> To the holy city of Byzantium.

The voyage to Byzantium becomes a quest for adequate compensation when the speaker, imaging his physical self as a scarecrow, characterizes the soul as obscuring the decrepitude of the body by increasing the volume of its song, which is a curious way of asserting the greatness of intellect and art. The difference, one would expect, between the song of the body and the song of the soul is qualitative. But by his loving recall of the sensual in the first stanza Yeats generated more tension in his poetic statement than my prose summary could possibly suggest. He insists too much that the mind is greater than the body. His quasi-Platonic scheme—the "unageing intellect" versus "whatever is begotten, born, and dies"—suggests a contrast between the real and the illusory in the first stanza, but this scheme becomes ludicrous when the so-called real (the soul) is placed in a hysterical shouting match with the illusion (the body). The conclusion of the second stanza has the force of suggesting that Platonic schemes are invalid in the world of process, and that the Manichean view (a philosophy of antinomy, so to speak) of two equally powerful and opposed forces which are unresolved is more appropriate. And therefore the old man will sail out of time and go to the "holy city" where the antinomic view of reality is inoperative, where the soul is king.

> O sages standing in God's holy fire
> As in the gold mosaic of a wall,
> Come from the holy fire, perne in a gyre,
> And be the singing masters of my soul.
> Consume my heart away; sick with desire
> And fastened to a dying animal
> It knows not what it is; and gather me
> Into the artifice of eternity.

The last two stanzas are set in the Byzantium of the old man's imagination, a place willfully conjured by the mind, not a place achieved in religious transformation. The point is delicately distinguished by the poet's rhetoric of invocation and prayer—"come," "consume," "gather"—which implies that the speaker is in a state of anxiety and need, rather than in a state of resolution. The will to identify the imaginative reality with true spiritual reality is poignantly articulated by the use of simile rather than metaphor: "O sages standing in God's holy fire / As in the gold mosaic of a wall." The naturalistic world cannot be understood by the concept of *figura*, or total metaphor; the formal statement of comparison emphasizes the disparity of words and things, of the gold mosaic and the spiritual realm, and the separateness as well as the likeness of the two things compared. From the harmony of the holy fire, the sages are asked to descend spinning into the chaos of history, an idea suggested by Yeats's metaphor of the gyre, his representation of the whirlpool-like nature of reality. The last four lines of the stanza turn us back to the pun on "dying generations." Being "sick with desire" (because he cannot "die" metaphorically?), his dying is literal. Furthermore, the request to be gathered into the "artifice of eternity" is as ambiguous as

105

"dying." Artifice suggests, of course, making in art, but it can imply, also, trickery or subterfuge, in which event the old man is fully aware of the compensatory nature of his quest. And there is another kind of ambiguity here, this one generated by the syntax of the phrase "artifice of eternity." Is the work of art "permanent" because it is made by eternity's artist? Or, is the work of art a mere fiction, a feigning of eternity? Sympathetically seen, the desire is to be transformed into an aesthetic image which participates in eternity; ironically seen, it is a request for aid to escape through artifice the antinomic nature of reality and the carrion of old age.

> Once out of nature I shall never take
> My bodily form from any natural thing,
> But such a form as Grecian goldsmiths make
> Of hammered gold and gold enamelling
> To keep a drowsy Emperor awake;
> Or set upon a golden bough to sing
> To lords and ladies of Byzantium
> Of what is past, or passing, or to come.

The tension and ambiguity implicit in the first three stanzas are here, in the last stanza of the poem, concentrated into a statement that points two ways and chooses neither. Taking on unnatural form underscores the artist's desire to transcend the organic, but his role so transformed can be looked at in two ways: he is the transcendentally sanctioned prophet, yes, but his duty to keep a sleepy ruler awake is a pretty menial task— at best the artist is an entertainer, at worst an alarm clock. And though the composition of his body may be of "hammered gold" (suggesting great value), its form undercuts the desire for transcendence of the natural, for what is it but a bird that sits "upon a golden bough to sing"? The final line of the poem, though prophetic in intent, with its triadic syntax has the artist looking back to "fish, flesh, or fowl" and "begotten, born, and dies." [36] The voyage out of time, out of the organic, is heavily qualified; the resolution of the antinomies of time and eternity, self and soul, art and nature, is not achieved but is reestablished more emphatically than ever. Here, Yeats's criticism of Shelley and Valéry in *A Vision* is illuminating:

> He [Shelley] lacked the Vision of Evil, could not conceive of the world as a continual conflict, so, though great poet he certainly was, he was not of the greatest kind.

❋ ❋

> Paul Valéry in the *Cimetière Marin* . . . rejoices that human life must pass. I was about to put his poem among my sacred books, but I cannot now, for I do not believe him. [37]

From Yeats's point of view, Valéry had resolved the antinomy by embracing the flux, and Shelley had resolved it by embracing stasis. "Sailing to Byzantium" begins by questing in a Shelleyan manner, but ends by looking back into Valéry's world. Yeats's poem is capable of extreme ironic contemplation, while neither Shelley's nor Valéry's is, for the latter two dissolve one world in order to assert the ultimate reality of another. Yeats wants it both ways.

"Byzantium," with its maddeningly qualified syntax, its repetition of images in shifting emphasis, and its unobtrusively modulated point of view, reads almost incoherently. Its development is not progressive or logical, but elliptical and qualitative in Kenneth Burke's sense. In the first Byzantium poem, Yeats gradually extracted the antithetical values implicit in the same image. Thus the bird of sensuality became the bird of the soul, and finally, in the conclusion, the bird of both sensuality and soul. In between there is some narrative binding. The later poem lacks narrative binding, but the strategy of extracting the complex values of a given figure is basic to both poems.[38]

> The unpurged images of day recede;
> The Emperor's drunken soldiery are abed;
> Night resonance recedes, night-walkers' song
> After great cathedral gong;
> A starlit or a moonlit dome disdains
> All that man is,
> All mere complexities,
> The fury and the mire of human veins.

Like "Sailing to Byzantium," "Byzantium" begins by establishing a strong contrast. Here, the contrast between the world of the senses and the world of the mind is elaborated as a tension between the human and the superhuman (both paradoxically figured in "cathedral gong"—a signal of time, an emblem of eternity), between the unpurged images of day and those pure images of night, that is, between the aesthetic purity of abstract artifice (the "dome") and the complexity and turmoil of the organic ("fury and the mire of human veins"). The unpurged (those unable to be abstracted to the harmony of art) are evoked by Yeats briefly, but very powerfully, through allusion to his poem "Nineteen Hundred and Nineteen":

> Now days are dragon-ridden, the nightmare
> Rides upon sleep: a drunken soldier
> Can leave the mother murdered at her door,
> To crawl in her own blood, and go scot free. . . .

In the context of "Nineteen Hundred and Nineteen" the "drunken soldiery" represent unbridled violence and disorder, mindlessness, destruction, and the forces of history—all in opposition to art, which is the manifestation of intellect in its search for order outside the process of history. In "Byzantium" the "drunken soldiery" contrast with the "dome" which, regardless of the play of natural light upon it, stands as a kind of thing-by-itself, an aesthetic order above human turmoil. "Night-walkers' song" stands in opposition to the "cathedral gong" which drowns it out, and "night-walker" may be a further reference to the unsavory soldiers or to what the soldier traditionally seeks when off duty. In any event, the soldiers and the night-walkers are parallel "unpurged images" standing in opposition to the "dome" of art especially, which "disdains" "all mere complexities."

The word "mere" seems to me especially well chosen. In its idiomatic sense it strengthens the contrast between art and man, deflates the significance of the human, just as sensuality, in the earlier poem, was deflated by "monuments of unageing intellect." The Platonic scheme implicit in the first stanza of "Sailing to Byzantium" was itself punctured as illusion when, later, the Manichean or antinomic sense of the world was developed. In "Byzantium," "mere" accomplishes this purpose in its root sense of "pure." Thus, the pure vitality of human mire and fury, the apotheosis of the organic, can be seen in Manichean opposition to the purity of execution in the Byzantine dome, the apotheosis of abstract creation. On the Platonic level, the dome, a transcendent aesthetic order, is reality, whereas the messy human life beneath is the illusion; but if we read "mere" for its other value, human complexity is as real and as powerful as aesthetic purity, and the two together make a dualism of pure opposites.

> Before me floats an image, man or shade,
> Shade more than man, more image than a shade;
> For Hades' bobbin bound in mummy-cloth
> May unwind the winding path;
> A mouth that has no moisture and no breath
> Breathless mouths may summon;
> I hail the superhuman;
> I call it death-in-life and life-in-death.

The first stanza has a "realistic" setting, ostensibly historical Byzantium. The second stanza, with its far-out imaginative conjurings, lacks such ballast. We cannot be sure what the poet knows, and he suggests as much

109

by his own qualifications. What is figured in the image of the "mummy"? Is it a man? No, more like a ghost. And, yet, more image than ghost. What Yeats sees here, I think, is an image of the artist who has already been gathered "into the artifice of eternity," abstracted to the state of Byzantium. The concluding lines of "All Souls' Night" suggest further that the mummy was emblematic to Yeats of creative thought itself and its embodiment in the work of art:

> Such thought, that in it bound
> I need no other thing,
> Wound in mind's wandering
> As mummies in the mummy-cloth are wound.

Generally, I believe this stanza is an attempt to articulate the opposition of the human and the superhuman, life and art, which was presented in the first stanza of "Byzantium." The feeling is of a mind reaching out, trying to grasp some truth in propositional form, but finally having to assert that the formulations of the imagination are subjective impositions of value and not objective breakthroughs to the truth: "more image than shade." That is, not a real spirit, but a spirit of the artificer's making.

"For Hades' bobbin bound in mummy-cloth / May unwind the winding path." As the image of the mummy floats down the street toward the narrator the poem reaches its ambivalent extremity. Like the monuments of the first Byzantium poem, the mummy can figure art's inability to participate in the organic vitality of life as well as its permanence, or even the artist's necessary but painful estrangement from life as well as the self-sufficiency of art ("in it bound / I need no other thing"). Again, the qualifier "may" and its repetition two lines later suggest the poet's agnostic attitude within a context of his own imagining. Though I disagree with F. A. C. Wilson's general view of Yeats— that he is a hidden doctrinal poet—his reading of "Hades' bobbin" seems cogent. Wilson identifies *The*

Republic as the source of the allusion and says that the
bobbin is the spool on which man's destiny is
wound.[39] The "winding path," suggestive of the gyre
metaphor evoked in the first Byzantium poem, describes, it seems to me, natural experience as a laby-
rinth. The two lines would suggest, then, that human
life is possibly resolved by art. The following two lines,
"A mouth . . . may summon," suggest an image of a
man anxiously in need of resolving great questions, but
responding to the answers of art ambivalently. In "Byzantium" that man is the poet brooding over his own
figures in search of something more deeply interfused.
There would seem to be little doubt that in loading
his poem with religious imagery Yeats would like to
say that art provides transcendental solace and meaning for tormented human existence. But the ironic
force of the concluding lines of the stanza severely
undercuts the possibility. Saluting his image as the
superhuman—literally, the more than human, that
which is beyond natural experience—the poet then
gives it diametrically opposed values. Like the paradox
of Keats's Grecian urn ("Cold Pastoral!"), the paradox
of the mummy is that it is at once a higher life, because great art endures down through the ages, and a
lower life, a kind of death, because art freezes human
vitality by imaging it.

> Miracle, bird or golden handiwork,
> More miracle than bird or handiwork,
> Planted on the star-lit golden bough,
> Can like the cocks of Hades crow.
> Or, by the moon embittered, scorn aloud
> In glory of changeless metal
> Common bird or petal
> And all complexities of mire or blood.

The third stanza condenses Yeats's double vision of
the relationship of art and organic nature. The superiority of art ("glory of changeless metal") over ever-
changing organic nature lies in art's freedom from the

complexities of natural life and its freedom from time. Insofar as the mind can immerse itself in the permanence of art, it immerses itself in a realm of aesthetic purity and order. Art can mock the impurity of nature and in this sense it is superhuman. The resolution of human fury is the "miracle" of art. And yet, though the artist may wish to lift his creation out of the flux, he cannot really do so. For the metallic, "changeless" bird, emblematic of the state outside nature which abstract art tries to create, is "embittered": the verb links art inseparably with those unpurged, organic images characterized by Yeats as "bitter furies." By describing the metallic bird in this way he brings his categories of opposition into ironic contact. (In "Sailing to Byzantium," we recall, the golden bird singing of time creates a similar effect.) The artifact does not permanently transcend nature, and the implication is that the resolutions of art are but fleeting, that the mortal world of "fish, flesh, or fowl" will not relinquish its claims on the maker.

> At midnight on the Emperor's pavement flit
> Flames that no faggot feeds, nor steel has lit,
> Nor storm disturbs, flames begotten of flame,
> Where blood-begotten spirits come
> And all complexities of fury leave,
> Dying into a dance,
> An agony of trance,
> An agony of flame that cannot singe a sleeve.

The speaker envisions, from here to the end, a dramatic collision of his antinomic images. The flames, like the metallic bird, stand outside nature because they are the flames of art ("that cannot singe a sleeve"), begotten by the flame of the creative imagination. The "blood-begotten spirits," those unpurged images of organic complexity, participate in the harmony of art by feeding themselves into the flames. At the crucial points, Yeats's best poems can go two ways; this stanza is one of those points. "Agony," like "mere" and the phrase "death-in-life and life-in-death," can suggest radically different meanings. What first comes to mind is the agony of ecstasy, the intense moment of religious realization, but in this context the moment of aesthetic resolution of the human condition. But the common meaning of the word—sheer pain and torture —is also relevant. If we allow Yeats his agnostic point of view, and the idea that this action is all taking place within a poetic mind uncertain of the values and meaning of its images, then the pressing question is: Where does the agony lie? If in the "blood-begotten spirits," then agony may be a prelude to aesthetic transcendence. If in the speaker, then Yeats is agonized because (as his endless qualifications might suggest) he cannot penetrate the meaning of his own images, because his own flame of imagination cannot singe sleeves.* As the Emperor, a figure for the poet, he finds his subjects (or images) a bit recalcitrant.

> Astraddle on the dolphin's mire and blood,
> Spirit after spirit! The smithies break the flood,
> The golden smithies of the Emperor!
> Marbles of the dancing floor
> Break bitter furies of complexity,
> Those images that yet
> Fresh images beget,
> That dolphin-torn, that gong-tormented sea.

In the final stanza the question of the relationship of the creative imagination ("golden smithies") and the sea of humanity, and the implied question of the relationship of art ("marbles") and nature (the spirits riding the sea waves on dolphins' backs), are left unresolved. Even while art "breaks" the organic, the cycles of birth and death continue. Here, in "Byzantium," is more than the finely balanced ironic vision of "Sailing to Byzantium." There, Yeats could look two ways at

* With all their theoretical insistence upon the free, nonutilitarian imagination, modern poets often express the desire in their poems for an imaginative power that will effect change in the world of action.

once; now he exalts both the tremendous vitality of natural life and the abstracted harmonies of art in equally energetic tones. As the "bitter furies" of the "gong-tormented" world get broken into order ("dance"), Yeats turns, in the last line, to the sea of finite experience which is haunted and pained (agony, perhaps, is the word) by the antinomic human condition. The state of Byzantium can exist psychically, at times, but never permanently, for the order created by the imagination is itself continuously being broken by the flood of nature's mire and blood. To go back, now, to that passage from *A Vision*, can we say with any confidence that the "philosophical worker in mosaic . . . could answer all my [Yeats's] questions"?

BEYOND BYZANTIUM: "LAPIS LAZULI"

The Byzantium poems are the culminating effort to resolve in poetry the problem of the relationship of art to nature and of a transcendent realm to a purely naturalistic one. As Yeats formulated the problem in the earlier poems as well as in the Byzantium poems, the antinomic categories are mutually exclusive, and the irony of the Byzantium poems, so thorough and so pervasive, seems to deny resolution by way of aesthetic transcendence. With the voyage to Byzantium stalled somewhere in the symbolic seas, and with a return trip to "that country" imminent, if not desirable, the problem of the artist has to be put on different grounds. If not Byzantium, what then?

In comparison with Yeats's Byzantium poems, "Lapis Lazuli" is not difficult. What has given the critics trouble is the poem's progression and design, the relationships of the larger parts. The problem taken up here is approximately the same one Yeats took up in his theoretical writings after 1903. How does the artist retain creative freedom once he has accepted the naturalistic scheme of things, there being no alternative, and has immersed himself in history? How does the artist reject idealistic and magical theories of poetry without being subject to naturalistic determinism? Yeats suggests that the human will alone can collapse, for a moment, the denial of freedom implicit in naturalism. And it does so in the making of art. Answers to how and why are offered by his later prose writings. "Lapis Lazuli," a later poem, does not simply mirror Yeats's theory of immersed self and impersonality, but goes beyond to present the felt experience of the artist paradoxically creating in a world that beats him down along with his art and his civilization.

> I have heard that hysterical women say
> They are sick of the palette and fiddle-bow,
> Of poets that are always gay,
> For everybody knows or else should know
> That if nothing drastic is done
> Aeroplane and Zeppelin will come out,
> Pitch like King Billy bomb-balls in
> Until the town lie beaten flat.

The poem begins by relating some familiar gossip about the socially irresponsible artist who goes his own way, regardless of the concrete, traumatic happenings in the real world. The hysterics want the artist to change his ways and to do something about the war and their world, which they feel is going to pieces. The tone of the speaker, however, tips his attitude: he is indeed "gay" (as charged), and it comes through in his description of an air raid: "Pitch like King Billy bomb-balls in." The poet, by putting the terrible event in the lingo of the sportsman describing his favorite game (pitch baseballs, footballs, etc.), rejects the plea of the women.

> All perform their tragic play
> There struts Hamlet, there is Lear,
> That's Ophelia, that Cordelia;
> Yet they, should the last scene be there,
> The great stage curtain about to drop,

If worthy their prominent part in the play,
Do not break up their lines to weep.
They know that Hamlet and Lear are gay;
Gaiety transfiguring all that dread.
All men have aimed at, found and lost;
Blackout; Heaven blazing into the head:
Tragedy wrought to its uttermost.
Though Hamlet rambles and Lear rages,
And all the drop scenes drop at once
Upon a hundred thousand stages,
It cannot grow by an inch or an ounce.

The second strophe is a view of death and the human will. Going much further than the hysterical women, Yeats says that not Ophelia alone, but all human beings are tragic figures made so by the fact of individual extinction. Furthermore, Yeats hypothesizes, even if total annihilation were at hand, even if the tragic setting—our world—were about to blow up, the great death would still be just the great death, as Stephen Crane's hero in *The Red Badge of Courage* found out. Why? Because, Yeats suggests, man possesses total freedom and can laugh in the very midst of tragedy, and no external law can possibly keep him from this ultimate expression of the autonomy of his will. Traditionally this has been called "tragic joy," the hero's rising above evil fortune and circumstance. Here, in "Lapis Lazuli," builders are seen as creative artists, and creative artists as tragic heroes who triumph over the tragic setting, not by seeking transcendence of a space-time world through imaginative perception, but by cutting themselves loose in the very process of their craft:

On their own feet they came, or on shipboard,
Camel-back, horse-back, ass-back, mule-back,
Old civilizations put to the sword.
Then they and their wisdom went to rack:
No handiwork of Callimachus,
Who handled marble as if it were bronze,

116

Made draperies that seemed to rise
When sea-wind swept the corner, stands;
His long lamp-chimney shaped like the stem
Of a slender palm, stood but a day;
All things fall and are built again,
And those that build them again are gay.

Yeats here extends the tragic fate to whole civilizations, works of art included; everything must go
through the process of birth, decay, and death. The
emblem of the artist as Callimachus is particularly relevant to the concept of the poetics of will discussed
above: he is seen as the stonecutter who makes through
shaping and carving, but whose painstaking efforts
must be inevitably annihilated. The important thing
seems to be to know that the aesthetic achievement is
ephemeral, doomed to time, but to engage in creation
anyway. Again it seems to me that such making and
building, in the face of sure extinction, is what Yeats
stresses throughout the poem because creativity symbolizes the freedom of the artist within a deterministic
framework. "And those that build them again are gay"
because they are free, and they are free because they
are creative. To laugh at tragedy, or to make poems in
the face of it, cannot defeat tragedy, but it can provide
a momentary release.

Two Chinamen, behind them a third,
Are carved in lapis lazuli,
Over them flies a long-legged bird,
A symbol of longevity;
The third, doubtless a serving-man,
Carries a musical instrument.

Every discoloration of the stone,
Every accidental crack or dent,
Seems a water-course or an avalanche,
Or lofty slope where it still snows
Though doubtless plum or cherry-branch
Sweetens the little half-way house

Those Chinamen climb towards, and I
Delight to imagine them seated there;
There, on the mountain and on the sky,
On all the tragic scene they stare.
One asks for mournful melodies;
Accomplished fingers begin to play.
Their eyes mid many wrinkles, their eyes,
Their ancient, glittering eyes, are gay.

The long-legged bird described in the scene carved
in stone is particularly functional; it is not a symbol of
the timeless (Byzantium), but of that which is subject
to process ("that country"). After contemplating the
artifact, Yeats, like Pope in the "Essay on Criticism,"
practices his theory. Though itself subject to process—
"Every discoloration . . . / Every accidental crack"
—the content of the image on the lapis lazuli is static.
But Yeats's free imagination, by playing upon the lapis
lazuli, changes it and makes poetry: "and I / Delight
to imagine them seated there." Yeats delights, though
the world is tragic, and the Chinamen delight at the
performance, though the melody is mournful. It is free
creation, however, which brings delight: for Yeats in
the making of poetry; for the Chinamen in the witnessing of a musical performance. Creation and gaiety
compose the confluence that explains how freedom is
achieved and how dread is briefly transfigured within a
naturalistic world. And not only the artist, but those
who can experience art, may in time itself enjoy the
momentary release from tragic necessity.

5

The Explicit Poetics of Wallace Stevens

When a poet makes his imagination the imagination of other people, he does so by making them see the world through his eyes. Most modern activity is the undoing of that very job. The world has been painted; most modern activity is getting rid of the paint to get at the world itself. . . . About escapism: Poetry as a narcotic is escapism in the pejorative sense. But there is a benign escapism in every illusion. The use of the word illusion suggests the simplest way to define the difference between escapism in a pejorative sense and in a non-pejorative sense: that is to say: it is the difference between elusion and illusion, or benign illusion. Of course, I believe in benign illusion. To my way of thinking, the idea of God is an instance of benign illusion. . . .

Letters of Wallace Stevens, p. 402

One evening, a week or so ago, a student at Trinity College came to the office and walked home with me. . . . I said that I thought that we had reached a point at which we could no longer really believe in anything unless we recognized that it was a fiction. The student said that that was an impossibility, that there was no such thing as believing in something that one knew was not true. It is obvious, however, that we are doing that all the time. . . . Of course, in the long run, poetry would be the supreme fiction.

Letters of Wallace Stevens, p. 430

WHEN in 1951 Wallace Stevens spoke at the National Book Awards, he made a few remarks about theory of poetry which were unmistakable in meaning:

Sir Walter Scott's poetry is like the scenery of a play that has come to an end. It is scenery that has been trucked away and stored somewhere on the horizon or just a little below. In short, the world of Sir Walter Scott no longer exists. It means nothing to compare a modern poet with the poet of a century or more ago.[1]

The romantic poetic is no longer viable because the idealistic theory of reality—Scott's view of the world—has ceased to be meaningful to us; Stevens suggested as much at the 1955 National Book Awards when he said that the poet of today "lives in the world of Darwin and not in the world of Plato."[2] Comments like these have been passed by as insignificant, apparently, because most of Stevens' critics see him as a theoretical romantic. The simple point that needs to be made is that Stevens is not a Coleridgean. In Stevens' own words the function of the modern poet is "to find, by means of his own thought and feeling, what seems to him to be the poetry of his time as differentiated from the poetry of the time of Sir Walter Scott, or the poetry of any other time."[3]

In this chapter I am guided by the assumption that Stevens' poetic cannot be defined in an essential way by his nineteenth-century inheritance in literary theory. In the process of probing for his modernity certain troublesome questions seem to demand our response: What does it mean to call him a romantic? a symbolist? a naturalist? The very asking should drive us back to the core conceptions offered in chapter 2. As I see it, however, finding answers for the questions is but half the task, which can be completed only by seeking further for Stevens' contributions to literary theory. My organization originates in his suggestion that he lives in Darwin's world and not in Plato's. The first part of this chapter is an analysis of Stevens' naturalistic orientation against the backdrop of the romantic inheritance he cannot accept; in the second part

I explore first his view of the nature of the imagination, and then his view of the relationship of imagination and medium; in the third part I attempt to isolate his understanding of the poetic context with relation to symbolist theories; and the last section is an account of his theory of poetic value, which means primarily a theory of the necessity of imagination and metaphor.

STEVENS' NATURALISTIC BASE

The suggestion that Stevens' temperament and theory of poetry are naturalistically based does not fit most current critical concepts of the poet. We understand that naturalism as a literary movement means the novel, and more specifically, novels like those of Émile Zola, Frank Norris, Theodore Dreiser, or James T. Farrell. Stevens wrote no fiction, of course, and we need only glance at his poetry to know that it is not in any ordinary sense "realistic." The idea of naturalism can be a meaningful one, however, if we consider it (as I have in chapter 2) philosophically (1) as a materialistic view of reality and (2) as a deeply skeptical attitude toward any theory of poetry wherein the imagination is given unique cognitive or constructive powers. To see naturalism in this way is to see it as a position antithetical to the core of neo-Kantian as well as romantic thought. Applied to Stevens' theoretical writings, the antithesis does not, unfortunately, illuminate all those elusive and involuted passages in his prose, but it does take us quickly to the theoretical issues that bothered him most.

The theme of time, process, flow, and decay is a pervasive one in Stevens' poetry,[4] and no less so in his essays where the naturalistic world view becomes a basis for his theory of poetry:

> To see the gods dispelled in mid-air and dissolve
> like clouds is one of the great human experiences.
> It is not as if they had gone over the horizon to

disappear for a time; nor as if they had been over-come by other gods of greater power and pro-founder knowledge. It is simply that they came to nothing. Since we have always shared all things with them and have always had a part of their strength and, certainly, all of their knowledge, we share likewise this experience of annihilation. It was their annihilation, not ours, and yet it left us feeling that in a measure, we, too, had been anni-hilated. It left us feeling dispossessed and alone in a solitude, like children without parents, in a home that seemed deserted, in which the amical rooms and halls had taken on a look of hardness and emptiness. What was most extraordinary is that they left no mementoes behind, no thrones, no mystic rings, no texts either of the soil or the soul. It was as if they had never inhabited the earth.[5]

Behind the passage lies the shattering impact of Dar-win, Marx, and Freud on modern thought. There is more here, however, than an abstract, academic under-standing of the history of ideas since 1859. What emerges from the passage is a personally felt aware-ness of isolation, loss, and the finality of time which is alien to Coleridge's feeling for the harmony of self and nature. As an existentialist might have put it, the face of reality has become irrational, enigmatic, and man confronts nature now, not as the continuum of self, but as the "other." Epistemologically, the end of romantic idealism heralds the death of the organic rec-iprocity of imagination and nature. The self that used to be understood as a manifestation of spirit is but a discrete and insignificant particular since its transcen-dent projection has been shorn away, or "annihilated," as Stevens wrote. The idealistic universe is dead.

In an essay uncharacteristically marked by social and political sensitivity, Stevens alluded to World War II with the familiar Darwinian image of struggle. He saw the conflict the world was witnessing as "only a part of a warlike whole," and he found particularly frightening, not the absence of spirit or the gods, as he put it—that was a matter for the classroom—but the immediate and unremitting pressure of war on the individual consciousness:

> Coleridge and Wordsworth and Sir Walter Scott and Jane Austen did not have to put up with Napoleon and Marx and Europe, Asia and Africa all at one time. It seems possible to say that they knew of the events of their day much as we know of the bombings in the interior of China and not at all as we know of the bombings of London. . . .[6]

The impact on Stevens of what he called the "pressure of reality," in a political and sociological sense, as well as in a philosophical one, is unmistakable even though the China reference is no longer effective. Clearly one "era in the history of the imagination"[7] (the romantic) had ended and a new one had begun.

In our time, idealistic views of the theory of knowledge become precious relics. Subject and object are not spiritually continuous, but are separated by an unbridgeable chasm. Stevens held[8] that the self-existent and self-explanatory world of matter stands alone, independent of our perception of it; thus, the act of dynamic imaginative perception of reality is not the center of the highest act of knowledge as it was for Coleridge. The stuff of knowledge is the stuff of external reality, an "objective" given, and one "knows" by observation, compilation, hypothesis, and, finally, by empirical verification of one's hypothesis. As Ernst Cassirer has put it, the singular goal of the logical positivist (a latter-day naturalist) in epistemology is to try to reproduce "the true nature of things as they are."[9] Obviously mind and language, in the positivist's view, are only passive (secretarial) instruments for recording and checking the truth, not instruments for making and shaping it. In Darwin's world "truth" is the inherent value of the "real." As Stevens puts it, "All our ideas come from the natural world"; "The ultimate value is reality." [10] And as the common-sense naturalist: "Kant says that the objects of perception are conditioned by the nature of the mind as to their form. But the poet says that, whatever it may be, *la vie est plus belle que les idées.*" [11] These are some of Stevens' naturalistic biases, and they extend to his view of poetry and the imagination:

> He [the poet] finds that as between these two sources [of poetry]: the imagination and reality, the imagination is false, whatever else may be said of it, and reality is true: and being concerned that poetry should be a thing of vital and virile importance, he commits himself to reality, which then becomes his inescapable and ever-present difficulty and innamorata. . . . He has strengthened himself to resist the bogus. [12]

One expects such statements from the hard-nosed naturalist, who looks at all idealistic views of mind as the useless theories of those who have not had the good fortune to be naturalists, but not from a man who spent many of the important hours of his adult life writing poetry.

There is no real contradiction, however. When Stevens calls imagination "the bogus" he is not suggesting that the imagination is unimportant, but simply that it is not centrally involved with cognition. In his opinion, the cognitive activity in man belongs exclusively to scientific and empirical method; the function of poetry must not be confused with the cognitive perception of truth. What is at issue here is the opposition between idealists and naturalists on mind's relationship to reality. Stevens, for example, explicitly denies the validity of the "metaphysical imagination" of the romantics, [13] a term he gets from Cassirer, because, as Cassirer put it in a passage that Stevens cites, [14] the romantic imagination claims to be the one avenue to ultimate reality and the source of all value. A romantic poem functions, finally, as an "opening" or a window to the structure of idealistic reality.

In the same passage in *An Essay on Man,* Cassirer made a further comment on the idealistic imagination of romanticism which underlines Stevens' own point of view:

> In order to achieve their metaphysical aim the romanticists had to make a serious sacrifice. The infinite had been declared to be the true, indeed the only, subject of art. . . . In this event what becomes of our finite world, the world of sense experience? Clearly this world has no claim to beauty. Over against the true universe [the idealistic universe], the universe of the poet and the artist, we find our common and prosaic world deficient in all poetic beauty.[15]

For Stevens the naturalist, the prosaic world of sense is the only world, and the one penetrated by the romantic imagination is an illusion. As for idealism's cognitive claims, he explicitly agrees with the positivist A. J. Ayer,[16] and says that they are literally nonsense because only propositions that are capable of being empirically verified have cognitive value. Here, in tho alliance with Ayer, is the unbridgeable gulf between the philosophical idealism of Coleridge and the philosophical naturalism of Stevens. Coleridge's world of spirit simply does not exist as far as Stevens feels he can know. The world of finite experience being everything, the values of an idealistic transparency of poetic form become something of a pleasant dream. No, Stevens will have nothing to do with romanticism: ". . . we must somehow cleanse the imagination of the romantic,"[17] he wrote, suggesting that for our time an adequate theory of imagination must take account of philosophical naturalism's redefinition of the context in which we live.

And yet, in spite of his naturalism, Stevens never hesitated to admit that he would happily embrace romantic theory were it intellectually honest to do so. A comment in an essay he wrote in 1951 indicates that he felt deeply the need for coherence and continuity: ". . . if we ignore the difference between men and the natural world, how easy it is suddenly to believe in the poem as one has never believed in it before, suddenly to require of it a meaning beyond what its words can possibly say." [18] Stevens desires to affirm the core belief of romanticism at the very moment that he denies its credibility; in his poems the romantic "dream" and the naturalistic "fact" become the polar coordinates of thematic conflict, over and over again. In his essays he seems to say between the lines: "Wouldn't it be pretty to believe in the romantic dream?"

In a naturalistic view of epistemology, and in a naturalistic world of materialistic process, how then is the poetic imagination framed? The answer is implicit in the question. The modern imagination feeds on empirical reality just as Wordsworth's fed on infinity. "In poetry at least the imagination must not detach itself from reality," [19] one of Stevens' notebook aphorisms reads. Similarly, Stevens paid John Crowe Ransom what he would consider the highest of compliments: "Mr. Ransom's poems are composed of Tennessee." [20] If, on the other hand, the imagination loses vitality and relevance as it ceases to immerse itself in the real, as Stevens suggested it would, and if the real is in constant flux, then the vital imagination, and the vital poetry, will always attach themselves to "a new reality." [21] Because the imagination by itself is not much, because it is bogus, or false, as he suggested, it "has the strength of reality or none at all." [22] Two lines from one of Stevens' late poems express the feelings of the poet who lives and creates in this posttranscendental universe:

> He never felt twice the same about the flecked
>   river,
> Which kept flowing and never the same way
>   twice . . .[23]

Within this world, new poems and only new poems
can embody the qualities of vitality and freshness demanded by the naturalistic basis of Stevens' poetic.[24]
The writing of new poems becomes a necessity, not essentially a way of knowing, but a way of living fully
and honestly within an ever-changing self that is
trapped by an ever-changing world of material flow.

Finally, I think, the import of Stevens' naturalistic
view of the imagination is concentrated in a question
he once posed: "Why should a poem not change in
sense when there is a fluctuation of the whole of appearance?"[25] The question is a rhetorical one, of
course, and suggests that the poem is significant only
insofar as it is located in the perceived world ("the
whole of appearance") and faithful to it. Stevens' theory of reality and his view of the creative process imply, in the last analysis, a flat disbelief in any theory of
poetry which assigns to the imagination a unique power of knowing in either a transcendental or even a
purely finite way. Predictably, when Stevens ap-
proached the problem of whether or not poetry has a
cognitive function as such, his naturalist theories and
attitudes offered him a solution. His major distinction
was not, as has often been maintained by recent neo-
Kantian critics, a distinction between poetry and science as two discrete and equally valuable modes of
knowledge, but a distinction between rational and empirical knowledge. The former he assigned to philosophy and the latter, not to science alone, but, curiously,
to poetry also. Now, if "poetic truth is an agreement
with reality," and reality is defined by flow or process,
then poetic "truth" cannot be static; in a world of perpetual change only the new poem, theoretically, can

"agree" with the shifting face of reality.[26] But, one might object, it has already been argued that the imagination is not a cognitive faculty. That is true: the imagination *by function* is not a cognitive faculty. The poet, unlike the scientist, does not pretend to give us a body of propositions that are capable of being verified. The "truth" of poems is their recognizable relationship to a particular space-time locus; genuine "modern" poetry, for Stevens, is always emblematic of a poet living in a (literally) godforsaken world, of a poet who draws on the particulars of place as a starting point* because he cannot draw on spirit. In a naturalistic universe, *materia poetica* (a favorite Stevens phrase) is found wholly within the limits of finitude: ". . . the real is only the base—but it is the base." [27]

THE GAIETY OF LANGUAGE: AN APPROACH TO ARTISTIC FREEDOM

For most of us the idea of naturalism raises inevitably the specter of deterministic materialism. John Tyndall, an enthusiastic propagandist for Darwin, evoked that specter in classic terms when he said that "all our philosophy, all our poetry, all our science, all our art— Shakespeare, Newton, Raphael—are potential [pre-exist] in the fires of the sun." [28] Basically, and most destructively, deterministic materialism denies the artist creativity because it denies him freedom. All along, Stevens (like Yeats) was aware of this tyrannizing force within his own naturalistic vision. All along, he recognized that his deeply felt commitment to the unresolved universe of particulars, his love for things as they are, could conceivably destroy him as a poet by enslaving

---

* Our critical language is, unfortunately, deeply indebted to mimetic views of poetry. Let me emphasize, then, that I do not say that Stevens sees the poem as window to the naturalistic world. The "particulars of place" are only a starting point. In the following section I consider the problem in detail.

him to a secretarial function. Stevens neither fought the battle with Darwin nor accepted the theoretical position of Zola. He simply assumed that the act of writing poems was a free act, and that the poem itself did not represent a metrical dictation that the poet had recorded while listening to nature.[29]

"The Irrational Element in Poetry," an essay never published in his lifetime, is Stevens' text on freedom. Characteristically, the essay does not represent an engagement in dialectics for the purpose of "proving" a point. Stevens does not argue for freedom; he just asserts it. It is not easy to grasp his conception of freedom in this essay, not because of the lack of coherent argument, however, but because of the lack of transitional thought. He writes of the imagination, for example, as an "irrational element," and he defines the "irrational" not as psychological aberration, but simply as that "which takes place unaccountably."[30] The logic that we are supposed to sense running through his elliptical presentation might be summarized in this way: the imagination is free precisely because it is irrational; that is, it is not simply a function of external nature, or a function of the Freudian "personality." The imagination is an energy (not a faculty) that apparently demands to be grounded in a medium in which it may express its own irrational will. It is for this reason, I suppose, that Stevens says the "irrational" is found "wherever poetry is found."[31] The poem itself, then, as the objective embodiment of irrational poetic energy, becomes (as it does in Yeats) the symbol of the free imagination working within a context of reality which Stevens' naturalism defines as a context of materialistic necessity.

We come now to Stevens' dual (and somewhat paradoxical) resolve to requite the love of his "ever-present innamorata"—the world of finite experience—and to jilt her at the same time, because only in the jilting is the irrational imagination free to exercise its own prerogatives in the making of poems. "The Noble Rider and the Sound of Words," published about five years after "The Irrational Element in Poetry" was written, explains how Stevens fused the idea of free imaginative play with his naturalistic valuation of the real world. A poem, he wrote, is a conjunction of imagination and reality. But if reality is allowed to neutralize imaginative energy by exerting full pressure "on the consciousness to the exclusion of any power of contemplation," then the poem created will be an "absolute fact," a poem without imagination, and hence no poem at all.[32]

Stevens' contrast of the two functions of language sheds more light on his thinking. In his view, the *denotative* function of language is "favorable to reality" and to Zola's ideal of constructing a window of literary form which will look out upon the "truth" of a world of natural objects and experience.[33] For the dogmatic naturalist the denotative function of language is its truly valuable function: indispensable, in fact, in the cognitive process of reproducing, as Cassirer said, the "true nature of things as they are." As Stevens emphasized, however, the imagination is the "bogus" in theory of knowledge; it is neither a faculty for the perception of transcendent truth, nor is it peculiarly equipped to offer a body of propositional truths about the naturalistic universe. Transcendental truth was the province of the no longer believable romantic idealists; propositional truth belonged to the logical positivists.

As Stevens saw it, the modern imagination's cognitive role is a fake—"false," as he put it. Its true, virile role is to express its own innate energies and, in so doing, shape a poetic (not a propositional) discourse. Only when language is functioning in its *connotative* or "irrational" form, to link thoughts from two different essays, is it functioning favorably to the imagination.[34] The beginning of the act of poetry meant for Stevens the channeling of his irrational poetic energy into a language that simply windowed a world of natural objects. In the writing, the playing with his medium, imaginative energy is released and connotation is generated. The poem itself becomes not an opening or a transparency of form, but a context of language within which image and metaphor, diction and tone, exert reciprocal pressures that create the ironies, the ambiguities, and the multiple meanings that characterize the best of Stevens' poems. The system of linguistic interrelations within the poem is itself the poem. "Poetry," as he wrote, "*is* the gaiety (joy) of language." [35] Stevens' dual obsessions are reconciled: by beginning in natural fact, in purely referential images of experience, he satisfies his commitment to the deromanticized material universe; by releasing his "unaccountable" poetic energy he meets the demands of his imaginative impulses and allows himself the freedom to do with his world what he wills in the wit of his language.

STEVENS AND SYMBOLIST THEORY

In suggesting that Stevens views the poem as a special kind of discourse whose coherence and meaning may be identified as a system of interrelated verbal effects, I have raised implicitly the question of his relationship to symbolist theories of poetic value. Briefly, the question is whether or not the playing off of connotation and denotation creates a poetic entity that is like a "new nature," not about the real, but, in Ernst Cassirer's terms, constitutive of the real. Once again, here is that germinal passage from Kant's *Critique of Aesthetic Judgment* which has flowered in symbolist theory:

> . . . by an aesthetical Idea I understand that representation of the Imagination which occasions much thought without, however, any definite thought, i.e. any *concept,* being capable of

131

being adequate to it; it consequently cannot be completely compassed and made intelligible by language. . . . The Imagination . . . is very powerful in creating another nature, as it were, out of the material that actual nature gives it.[36]

As an utterly unique discourse, a self-enclosed cosmos of words—in Kant's phrase, "another nature"—the poem is a vehicle of a special kind of knowledge and value, neither propositional and scientific, nor transcendent and romantic. The neo-Kantians, with all their differences allowed for, have one purpose in common: to reinstate in terms particularly palatable to the agnostic modern mind, the autonomous cognitive power of the literary imagination. They have done so by ingeniously erecting an epistemology and an aesthetics on hints from Kant; man's symbolic forms of expression—art works, for example—are not "imitations of reality," Cassirer theorized,

> but organs of reality, since it is solely by their agency that anything real becomes an object for intellectual apprehension, and as such is made visible to us. The question as to what reality is apart from these forms, and what are its independent attributes, becomes irrelevant here. For the mind, only that can be visible which has some definite form; but every form of existence has its source in some peculiar way of seeing, some intellectual formulation and intuition of meaning.[37]

Art, Cassirer concluded, is no less important and no more important than science because, like science, it is "a particular way of seeing, and carries *within itself its particular and proper source of light*. . . . it is not a question of what we see in a certain perspective, but of the perspective itself" (italics mine).[38] In essence, Cassirer gives us a pluralistic universe in which man's various categories of thought, expression, and apprehension are themselves the autotelic forms through which the different aspects of reality are posited, condi-

132

tioned, and thus "seen" and "known." Each of the symbolic forms articulates a "myth," a coherently organized account of the world and our experience in it, and, put together, the myths give us (ideally) a portrait of human culture.

There are a number of ways to gauge Stevens' reactions to neo-Kantian literary theory, but none of them yields exact evidence of his thoughts because he never wrote directly to the issues. A few things become clear, however, if we contrast neo-Kantian theory with the framework and temper of Stevens' thought. For example, Kant's statement about the imagination creating "another nature" might be compared with a statement from Stevens which carries diametrically opposed import: "The imagination is able to *manipulate* nature as by creating three legs and five arms but it is *not able to create a totally new nature . . .*" (italics mine).[39] The manipulative imagination exercises its full power in the linguistic medium, but on existing "natures" or empirical entities, whereas the symbolist, constructive imagination "creates" in language new entities from raw materials.

The point and its ramifications are implicit in Stevens' naturalism: given that reality is self-existent and self-explanatory, man's symbolic forms do not, obviously, constitute it. Reality has fully formed, independent attributes prior to our perception of it; truth is objective, inherent in the self-existing real; and the best thing we can do to perceive truth is to neutralize the individuality of our perspectives. In a naturalistic conception of reality, only scientific method is properly equipped for the cognitive process because only scientific method employs language dispassionately for the sake of reality.[40] Language for the scientist is useful only in its purely referential, denotative, or transparent function. Whether or not words can ever perform this way, Stevens and a certain school of modern philosophy seemed to think so. Stevens, and the positivists with him, saw the poetic imagination as the "bogus" in the act of knowledge (not a unique cognitive faculty) because the imagination, by its very nature, is incapable of using language in its function as a representation of reality. The imagination can neither perceive nor make the truth but only manipulate it in the gaiety of language. In this manipulation, the play of irrational energy and connotation, the truth—nature as it is—is changed and distorted as poetic energy and poetic discourse satisfy their own standards of validity. The value of a poem is neither cognitive nor ontological but, quite by design, something else. "All the great things have been denied," Stevens wrote, "and we live in an intricacy of new and local mythologies, political, economic, poetic, which are asserted with an ever-enlarging incoherence." [41] The implication of Cassirerian thought, with its plurality of cognitive systems, seemed to dishearten the naturalistically persuaded Stevens, who believed that cognition was a scientific value and not an aesthetic one.

There yet remains the problem of Stevens' contextualism. The easy answer, of course, is that Stevens implicitly denies the contextual version of symbolist poetic for the simple reason that he denies the constructive imagination. For if we push hard enough on the organic ideal of contextualism, the inseparability of form and content, it is clear that Stevens' manipulative imagination is a form-giving faculty. A poem, in his view, may ultimately be broken down into its naturalistic base, its core referential image, and the metamorphic and distorting effects wrought by language on that image in the making of the poem. In comparison with the absolute organicism of contextualism, then, Stevens' conception of form is surely decorative because it implies an artist who is highly conscious of shaping his medium toward a particular end.

But, though absolute organicism may be an untenable idea, a sympathy toward the contextual attitude is a necessary part of Stevens' poetics. I take it that his comment, "above everything else, poetry is words," [42] indicates a symbolist emphasis in his theory of poetry. The value of the poem, however, is not inherent solely in the medium of the poem, but in our apprehension of that very distortion or metamorphosis that the poetic context has performed on its own naturalistic base. We must know the poetic context as a context before we can hold it up and compare its image with the reality outside. And to some degree we have to recognize that Stevens' highly stylized poems issue from a linguistic sleight of hand that attempts to disguise, by elaborate connotative effect, a denotative reference to a barren reality. Stevens' sense of symbolism is that a poem is primarily verbal; it is not the sense that a poem is a special cognitive organ, or a means of getting access to an otherwise inaccessible level of reality.

The Uses of Poetry

> It is a violence from within that protects us from a violence from without. It is the imagination pressing back against the pressure of reality. It seems, in the last analysis, to have something to do with our self-preservation; and that, no doubt, is why the expression of it, the sound of its words, helps us to live our lives.
>
> *The Necessary Angel*, p. 36

The immediate cause of poetry is the channeling of irrational, finite energy through the artistic will which then binds itself to language. Why does the poet write poetry, we might ask Stevens, and he answers: "A poet writes poetry because he is a poet." [43] It is a very honest answer, perhaps the only one possible considering his refusal to assign unique cognitive or prophetic powers to the imagination. I take it he means that a poet will use his gift even though he is not philosophically sanctioned as Mallarmé was, or as Blake was. But Stevens had other reasons for writing poetry, and he often spoke of them.

Poems are more than expressions of freedom within a deterministic universe: they serve a psychologically therapeutic purpose as well. The particular end toward which Stevens shapes and directs verbal effects is the "idea of order," a pleasing illusion in language which releases the poet from his barren and sometimes ominous circumstances. For the naturalistic flux can never satisfy the human hunger for permanence, or coherence, or the need to be lord of nature; nor can it give the greater reassurance—the deeper and final resolution—that we are fused to spirit, or God, or the One through nature. Poems must somehow fill the void: "In an age of disbelief . . . it is for the poet to supply the *satisfactions* of belief. . . . We do not say that the poet is to take the place of the gods" (italics added).[44]

Poems cannot give back to us our lost faith, nor can they reconstitute the unsatisfactory world for us in any lasting sense. But the poet may render in his medium willfully distorted images of the world which enable us to feel, briefly, how it might be to live in a world much better than the one we have. In a sense this is a highly sophisticated way of kidding oneself, but Stevens believes it a psychic necessity to play the game: "It seems, in the last analysis, to have something to do with our self-preservation." And that is why the poem is so important to us; in our posttranscendental world where death is god it can be the necessary illusion that locks out the violence of modern reality. We need images of coherence and permanence in a world that does not look at all like Wordsworth's and that threatens to make reasonably happy living impossible. Stevens' only admonition is that we recognize an aesthetic ordering—"the gaiety of language"—as merely linguistic. Accordingly, the honest poet and the honest reader will recognize that the poetic illusion is merely an illusion projected by artifice and not a penetration to a more deeply interfused ontological structure.

The prime motivation of the imaginative man, then,

most generally defined, is his need for order which he manifests in his constant "probing for an integration." The integration of self and nature on an idealistic scale would be the ultimate integration, but one that cannot, unfortunately, be forthcoming. Still, the habit of probing continues, writes Stevens, and "seems to be part of the general will to order." [45] In its irreducible modern function the imagination is very modest, and deluding, too, as his illustrations indicate: "It colors, increases, . . . says to women more than it is possible to say, it rescues all of us from what we have called absolute fact. . . ." [46] Stevens' examples are suggestive of his central idea. In an unresolved universe the imagination can help us, in his words, to "resist," "evade," and "escape" the "pressure of reality," [47] the monotony, the pain, and the horror of "absolute fact" which life offers us: "It [imagination] is part of our security. It enables us to live our own lives. We have it because we do not have enough without it." [48] Similar utterances make the point of the imagination's dire necessity: ". . . we live in . . . a geography that would be intolerable except for the non-geography [the constructs of will] that exists there." [49] It is the intolerable geography, the world as we know it in plain perception, which forces the mind, "in the absence of a belief in God," to turn to "its own creations . . . for the support they give." [50] The writing of poems becomes the last defense of the existential artist.

Clearly, it is not worthwhile to conceive of Stevens' views of the imagination and poetry in epistemological and ontological terms, because he just does not see things that way. In an essay entitled "Imagination as Value," he makes this rather astounding admission (in view of the title): "We are concerned with the extent of artifice within us and, almost parenthetically, with the question of its value." [51] Precisely this "extent of artifice," in the last analysis, may be identified as the value of imagination. Though Stevens cannot claim for

137

his view what the romantics and symbolists claimed for theirs, the imagination is now hardly less necessary than it was for Coleridge or Mallarmé. As my epigraph may suggest, it comes to a question of sanity, or if that is too strong, a question of emotional well-being at least. Asking himself directly about the function of the imagination in our time, Stevens bluntly wrote that we now turn to poetry for compensation and solace: "Men feel that the imagination is the next greatest power to faith. . . . their interest in the imagination . . . is . . . a vital self-assertion in a world in which nothing but the self remains, if that remains."[52] The poetic imagination cannot take the place of God and the Bible, but it is the "next greatest power to faith." In a world stripped of all idealistic value, self and nature are irrevocably split, the ambitious myths of poetry and religion have outlived their validity, and only the self remains. The situation is nothing short of desperate. A poet's imagination truly plays a vital role in our culture because it contributes to the individual's "self-preservation."

By repeatedly suggesting that the imagination does with reality "whatever it wills,"[53] Stevens reminds us, finally, that he must turn away from his own naturalistic propensities, or that in spite of them he will formulate a theory of imagination on irrational grounds,[54] thereby postulating aesthetic freedom within a deterministic context. This irrational energy of imagination, which "defends us against terror,"[55] does so by creating "fictions."[56] The word "fiction" has two senses in Stevens: one suggests "form" or "shape," an idea of order in which self and world are coherently organized; the other, simply that which is feigned, an illusion.[57] In Stevens' essays, and especially in his poems, the two meanings are amalgamated, for the imagination, as the weapon of will and desire, satisfies the needs of the impoverished self, not by penetrating or windowing a "higher" reality, nor by offering a unique form of knowl-

138

edge outside scientific method, but by defeating the chaos of reality with fictional orders generated by gaiety of language in the illusory *"mundo"* [58] of the poetic medium. "A possible poet," he wrote, "must be a poet capable of resisting or evading the pressure of . . . reality. . . ." [59] Why evade? Because one needs to; modern reality is not enough to make us happy, and the "purpose of poetry is to contribute to man's happiness." [60]

In the meaning of his concepts of "fiction," "abstraction," and "metaphor," Stevens concentrates what he sees as the value of poetic discourse. If it is true that he means to convey by such terms something of idealistic import, then it might be maintained that his view of imaginative value cannot be simply a response to the needs of will, as I have been suggesting. The "fiction," first of all, is a cultivated illusion made by the process of "abstracting," or consciously distorting the chaos of the real into a palatable image: "Resistance to the pressure of ominous and destructive circumstances consists of its conversion, so far as possible, into a different, an explicable, an amenable circumstance." [61] Distortion or abstraction is what this notebook aphorism refers to: "The poet makes silk dresses out of worms." [62] That is, the poet "abstracts" reality "by placing it in his imagination," which is a "disengaging of (a) reality," or, he might have said, a tearing of selected particulars from reality's context. [63]

Stevens' notion of "abstraction" appears to have an illuminating explanation in Paul Valéry, whose work he knew well, and for whose collected edition he wrote two prefaces. I doubt it accidental that the works that Stevens chose to preface, "Dance and the Soul" and "Eupalinos, or the Architect," have direct bearing on his own theory of poetry. In "Eupalinos," Valéry differentiates sharply between aesthetic creation and the creation of nature. In natural creation form and content are inseparable, that "which makes and that

139

which is made are indivisible." [64] The natural thing is defined by the reciprocity of form and matter. Aesthetic creation, however, is not organic, but artificial: "But as for the objects made by man, they are due to the acts of thought. The principles are separate from the construction, and are as it were imposed by a tyrant from without upon the material." [65] Valéry defines artificial, human creation with the word "abstraction": "Man, I assert, fabricates by abstraction, ignoring and forgetting a great part of the qualities of what he uses." [66] And how does this unnatural creation function? Valéry's answer could have been written by Stevens: it is an "expression of the needs and desires of man." [67] Aesthetic constructs are finally characterized by Valéry as "acts of the mind," [68] a phrase Stevens used in one of his famous poems, "Of Modern Poetry" (analyzed in chapter 6).

It ought to be said, because it often goes unsaid, that what Stevens learned from the great French symbolist poet was not a principle of symbolism. In symbolist theory the organic analogy is made *ad nauseam* in order to underscore the utter inviolability of the aesthetic object; the poem is a "world" quite literally in symbolist theory, a world of self-existing status. The aesthetic world functions like an organism in that it is both autonomous and autotelic. As Valéry and Stevens describe the creative process, however, the aesthetic object has no such independent stature. A poem is a consciously fabricated thing whose reasons for being are lodged deep in the poet's psyche. The process of abstraction is the poet's way of channeling his needs and desires into language: ultimately, an imposition of a fictive form or order on the disordered content of experience.

From this process of abstraction and manipulation come the "deliberate fictions" that Stevens, without hedging or embarrassment, called a likely forerunner to a "science of illusions." [69] These illusions have a certain vitality because the imagination, naturalistically grounded, immerses itself in the real to begin with. The value of the illusion is to give "life whatever savor it possesses," but this "savor" has its source in the gaiety of language (the "fiction") and not in the content of experience.[70] Here, in a central passage, Stevens ties together the notions of abstraction, fiction, and willed evasion:

> . . . the artist transforms us into epicures; . . . he has to discover the possible work of art in the real world, then to extract it, when he does not himself compose it entirely; . . . he is *un amoureux perpétuel* of the world that he contemplates and thereby enriches; . . . art sets out to express the human soul; and finally . . . everything like a firm grasp of reality is eliminated from the aesthetic field. With these aphorisms in mind, how is it possible to condemn escapism? The poetic process is psychologically an escapist process. The chatter about escapism is, to my way of thinking, merely common cant. My own remarks about resisting or evading the pressure of reality mean escapism, if analyzed. Escapism has a pejorative sense, which it cannot be supposed that I include in the sense in which I use the word. The pejorative sense applies where the poet is not attached to reality, . . . which, for my part, I regard as fundamental.[71]

Stevens gives here the essence of everything he said about the theory of poetry. He walks the line separating the purely "fictive" (the structure that is wholly imaginative), a defective poem,[72] from the purely "real," a surrender to unadulterated naturalism, the source of an equally defective poem. He begins where the naturalist begins, in the empirical world, but then he starts his transformations; he "extracts," or abstracts, as he is more apt to say, until the real has been dislocated and placed in the "bogus," the imagination.

This process is certainly a kind of escapism because it is a turning away from reality, or a distortion of reality, but it is not escapism in the worst sense, which means that the poet [73] begins and ends with the imaginative—the "false," as Stevens defined it.

The philosopher Stevens most admired, George Santayana, once said that in "prompting mankind to imagine, he [the poet] would be helping them to live." [74] Stevens suggested a similar idea when he said that the artist "transforms us into epicures," not, of course, by titillating the senses, but by abstracting in language a reality that rarely offers pleasure. Through the process of abstraction, the poet creates for us another "reality," an imaginative world, "a fictitious existence on an exquisite plane." [75] By entering the poet's imaginative perspective through his medium we enter his fictitious world and leave behind, for a while, the harsh naturalistic world. This is neither an effete, gutless view of poetry, nor a dishonest one. Once we allow Stevens his naturalistic view of reality and understand that he was not recommending that we simply delude ourselves, but that we delude ourselves and know that we do so because we must and because finally it comes to a question of survival, his conclusion is consistent: "The final belief is to believe in a fiction, which you know to be a fiction, there being nothing else, the exquisite truth is to know that it is a fiction and that you believe in it willingly." [76] And this has everything to do with the responsibility of the artist to society as a whole, though Stevens would never put it that way. He did put it this way: the poet searches for "some supremely acceptable fiction," [77] not because he is an "evangelist," [78] not because he is going to take the place of God, and his poetry the place of heaven, but because he is going "to make his own imagination that of those who have none, or little." [79] The one thing that makes the poet so powerful a figure is that "he creates the world to which we turn incessantly and without knowing it and . . . he gives to life the supreme fictions without which we are unable to conceive of it." [80]

Stevens' last suggestion is reminiscent of Oscar Wilde's essay, "The Decay of Lying." I cannot prove conclusively that Stevens knew this work, but the idea that we view reality through the eyes of imaginative writers is certainly a distinct parallel. Wilde's essay was written under the impact of French symbolism, and was buttressed by a revival of interest in German idealistic philosophy. Stevens is not Wilde; there is little reason to believe that the solipsism in Wilde's theorizing could ever be taken seriously by Stevens: "What the eye beholds may be the text of life. It is, nevertheless, a text that we do not write." [81] What Stevens suggests is that we prefer to look at life through the artist's eyes because we find it easier to take that way. This is a minimal "idealism," if that, and about all that we may safely attribute to him.

Stevens' ideas on metaphor, closely related to his theories of "fiction" and "abstraction," are worked out mainly in two essays: in the first part of "Three Academic Pieces" and in "Effects of Analogy." In the former Stevens begins by writing that empirical reality is poetry's central reference [82]—reminding us again of his naturalistic bias—but that in metaphor, the chief tool of the illusion-creating imagination, empirical reality is changed for the reader. He identifies both poetry and metaphor with metamorphosis, and metamorphosis is explained as the "creation of resemblance by the imagination." [83] Metaphor, according to Stevens, is the figure productive of metamorphosis, so metaphor becomes, for him, the vital figure in the language of poetry. [84] Now, what exactly does he mean when he says that reality is changed in metaphor? First of all, metaphor is like the fiction because it changes reality for the self and makes it more amenable by erecting a defense against disorder. Metaphor defends us because it remakes the perceived objects in the external world by taking them into a world of the mind: "The absolute object slightly turned is a metaphor of the object." [85] Another and more familiar function of metaphor (yet still a method of defense) is its power to change perceived reality for the reader by making resemblances and orders where none really exist. Through either function of metaphor, the poet creates one of those "fictions" that help us to live our lives: "Reality is a cliché from which we escape by metaphor. It is only *au pays de la métaphore qu'on est poète*." [86] Thus, metaphor, abstraction, and fiction all coalesce in Stevens in the idea of the calculated, artificial change which produces a satisfying illusion that transports us to the imagination's sweet country. Metaphor is a "satisfying of the desire for resemblance," [87] but to satisfy a desire for resemblance in metaphor is not, of course, to say that the resemblances are perceived, that the orderings of metaphor are discovered, but that they are subjectively created and imposed, that external reality is distorted in the poem because the poet needs order and it is not forthcoming from without: "What the eye beholds may be the text of life. *It is, nevertheless, a text that we do not write*. The eye does not beget in resemblance. It sees. But the mind begets in resemblance. . . . It is not difficult, having once predicated such an activity, to attribute it to a *desire* for resemblance" (italics mine). [88] Metaphoric orders are, finally, the required fantasies of the spiritually impoverished:

> One may find intimations of immortality in an object on the mantelpiece; and these intimations are as real in the mind in which they occur as the mantelpiece itself. Even if they are only part of an adult make-believe, the whole point is that the *structure of reality because of the range of resemblances that it contains is measurably an adult make-believe* [italics mine]. [89]

It follows that Stevens would define metaphor as "imaginative deviation," [90] a view that is not neo-

Kantian. In his latest book on the subject, *Metaphor and Reality*, Philip Wheelwright restates with unmistakable clarity what the neo-Kantian view of poetic language is: "Poetic language . . . partly creates and partly discloses certain hitherto unknown, unguessed aspects of What Is." [91] Again: ". . . the essential possibility of diaphor [an aspect of metaphor] lies in the broad ontological fact that new qualities and new meanings can emerge, simply come into being." [92] Wheelwright's idea that metaphor has a special capacity to constitute the real is far from Stevens' psychological, not ontological, emphasis on the resemblances created by desire.

What Stevens tries to suggest about metaphor—that it serves the will—is best illustrated in the analogy he makes with narcissism: ". . . Narcissus did not expect, when he looked in the stream, to find in his hair a serpent coiled to strike. . . ." [93] Of course, Narcissus found a handsome face, not a serpent. The beauty of Stevens' insight is in its obviousness: our self-projection into the external world is an act that gives us pleasure; the perception of our own glorified image in the pool of reality reduces reality to the familiar, that which can be encompassed in our own awareness, and thus ordered. ". . . Narcissism itself it merely an evidence of the operation of the principle that we expect to find pleasure in resemblances." [94] This, then, is the connection: metaphor is a self-satisfying method of ordering reality by the making of pleasing resemblances which do not exist outside the mind. We make a world without danger and chaos because that is the way we want it. We do not make worlds in which snakes are coiled to strike at every turn.

EPILOGUE

At the end of "The Future of an Illusion," a work that Stevens once cited with considerable contempt because of its arrogant positivism,[95] Freud remarks that it would be "an illusion . . . to suppose that what science cannot give us we can get elsewhere."[96] Freud's faith was total and unshakable at the time he wrote that essay; Stevens, much humbler in his naturalism, realized that science could satisfy only a small part of us and that the poetic imagination had to give us precisely what science was not equipped to give. But there is a point where the ideas of Stevens and Freud overlap; both see art as a response to a world less than satisfactory, neither assign cognitive or ontological powers to the imagination, and both see art as compensation.

Stevens might conceivably have written this section from "Civilization and Its Discontents":

Life, as we find it, is too hard for us; it brings us too many pains, disappointments and impossible tasks. In order to bear it we cannot dispense with palliative measures. . . . The substitutive satisfactions, as offered by art, are illusions in contrast with reality, but they are nevertheless psychically effective.[97]

Freud concluded that these illusions arise in the "life of the imagination,"[98] a phrase now commonly associated with Stevens. Like Freud's artist, Stevens' artist is a man who, as Stevens put it, "needed what he had created,"[99] and his audience needs it just as badly.

I would not care to push the Freud comparison very far. Stevens, after all, has no Oedipal complexes informing his poetic symbols. And more important than that, his assumption of a free imagination defies Freudian determinism. In the context of Stevens' thought, the psychological illusion is geared to the epistemologically repressed imagination, not the sexually repressed id. There is a sense in which his poetry, like Yeats's, is a poetry of conflict, but in Yeats the conflict is recognizable as dramatic experience, a "struggle of the individual and the world," as he put it. In Stevens

146

the dramatic encounter is intellectually enclosed: the mind, not the total self, encounters the world, and it is the mind in its act of finding what will suffice which requires a therapeutic illusion to protect it from the "violence from without," the face of modern reality. As a weapon of will and desire, the imagination attempts to supply what will suffice by making in the gaiety of language an illusion that momentarily brings peace to the mind. But the imagination's illusions are not accepted without reservation because the honest, self-questioning mind, the mind that can never be satisfied, knows that its imaginative constructions of order are only linguistically real, and that the modern imagination, in comparison with the epistemologically rich idealistic or neo-Kantian imagination, is impoverished. Finally, the modern mind is aware that the imagination is, because of its naturalistic frame, a purely finite instrument whose powers are limited to the artifices of the poetic medium. The mind requires more than that. With this acute understanding of the poverty and limits of his own theory, Stevens' poetry begins and his doctrine as doctrine ends.

6

Implicit Poetics and the Transmutation of Doctrine: Contexts of Key West

THE PRIMARY ASSUMPTION in Stevens criticism was accurately defined by the editors of *The Act of the Mind* when they said that they took him "seriously" as a "philosophical poet." Thus, in the romanticist interpretation, Harold Bloom places Stevens in the prophetic and apocalyptic mode, whereas the point of view epitomized by Joseph Riddel's *The Clairvoyant Eye* locates him as a modern humanist, passionately confident that the poetic imagination can take the place of transcendental aesthetic philosophies.[1] Neither point of view, it seems to me, is really justified by the poetry. For, no matter what theoretical position we assign Stevens, and no matter how well we define and substantiate it via his prose, the theoretical position alone is not adequate to the ironic tones of the poems. "I am not a philosopher,"[2] he wrote, meaning that he was not, as a poet, a systematic thinker or a consistent doctrinalist. But he certainly liked to toy with philosophical problems, especially epistemological ones. We need not worry too much about what constitutes sound or unsound responses to the questions posed by the theory of knowledge, since Stevens himself did not

148

mind admitting he learned his philosophy from a student handbook.[3] What happens, on the other hand, when philosophical ideas enter poems, and what characterizes a poet's exact tone and attitude toward these ideas, are matters for the critic.

I am not suggesting that Stevens' poems exist as poems because he dabbled, tongue in cheek, with philosophical ideas. He does often toy, but that is a manner of expression, a method, and not the heart of expression itself. And he does start with philosophical ideas, but that is his donée, the discursive matter he uses as the vehicle for the expression of his lyric impulses. For Stevens was not the kind of poet who could directly pour out his emotions; he needed doctrinal counters to which he could anchor the fundamental anguish and hopes of the self that could not be satisfied by its own theory of poetry. His poetic, it is true, did not allow for the prophetic, oratorical voice, but his poetic is only one term in the dialectical structures of his poems. The other term is that "tremendous statement," as R. P. Blackmur puts it,[4] which at bottom expresses the need to make tremendous statements, the nostalgic wish to say of the modern imagination's power so much more than the agnostic poet knows he should say—in fact, the wish to affirm the very things his aesthetic denies. The philosophical perspective is often the poem's perspective; irony is the poet's dominant tonality. But the two together do not add up to the poem, to the "gaiety of language" which is a linguistic rendering of the turmoil within the poetic mind that contemplates its own uncertain place in a century in which it has said "no" to the aesthetics and philosophy of romanticism.

In Stevens' poems what we might roughly call a Kantian epistemological position comes to life, not as a theoretical postulate, but as a poetic possibility, a part of a dialectic. For when Stevens was writing well, when he was able to get into his poems all the poetry of his subject as well as the bare doctrinal bones of that subject,[5] his work issues not in statement but in uneasiness of tone and the ambiguity of attitude of a man who had deeply irresolvable feelings about himself, the imagination, and the world he had to live in. And, I might add, his poems truly become poems as they are vitalized by his skepticism and irony. When the ironic eye blacks out, however, when the amateur philosopher crowds out the poet, they read like the monotonous expositions of an aesthetician who never had more than one or two ideas. At such times we can agree with Randall Jarrell that Stevens does sound like "G. E. Moore at the spinet."[6]

Kenneth Burke's definition of the ironist "as essentially impure, even in the chemical sense of purity," is here applicable. Burke's ironist "must deprecate his own enthusiasms, and distrust his own resentments,"[7] and Stevens measures up well because it is not essentially the Kantian idealism that invigorates his poems, but his "impurity," the curious doubleness and irresolution that are generated when he so severely undercuts his own desires. I have chosen to describe the form of Stevens' poems by the phrase "unresolved dialectic," by which I would convey the idea of tension between antithetical motivations. For example, the poet, after uttering "the final no" to all those doctrines of the imagination which the romantics and symbolists held, will then try to say "yes" to his own doctrine, and "yes" so resoundingly that he tries to make himself believe that his doctrine is as awesome as those of Mallarmé or Blake. In the confident oratory of "The Well Dressed Man with a Beard,"[8]

After the final no there comes a yes
And on that yes the future world depends.

But as the poem progresses, the oratorical tone diminishes, and the power of that "yes" diminishes with it as the probing skeptic realizes that the future world depends on something as fragile as a "cricket's horn," as mundane as a "petty phrase." The thing believed may not be rationally affirmed, only nostalgically longed for: "Ah! douce compagna of that thing!" The poem that begins with "yes" ends with "no": "It can never be satisfied, the mind, never."

"The Well Dressed Man with a Beard" will sustain patient analysis. I do not claim that I have done any more than point out that there are two dramatically contrasted voices in the poem which suggest two very different tones, two very different thematic emphases, two very different attitudes of the poet. The "yes" voice in Stevens is the voice of desire; the "no" voice is the factive, naturalistic voice. "No" does not overwhelm "yes"; it merely opposes. This is what I mean by an "unresolved dialectic" and I think Stevens' poems tend to work in that way. The first part of this chapter is an overview of the poems; the second part focuses on Stevens' considerations of metaphor and the constructive imagination; the last part is an analysis of "The Idea of Order at Key West," which I see as the symbolic center of his work.

The Ironic Eye

The experience most obsessively articulated in Stevens is the confrontation of world and self as the epistemological drama of perceiver and perceived. Whether it was imaginative perception, or just plain seeing through the naked eye which he was writing about, one term in his dialectic seemed to drive inevitably toward the position finally defined in his last long poem, "An Ordinary Evening in New Haven":

> If it should be true that reality exists
> In the mind: the tin plate, the loaf of bread on it,
> The long-bladed knife, the little to drink and her
> Misericordia, it follows that
> Real and unreal are two in one . . .[9]

The subjectivism so blatantly announced in these lines never sat well with Stevens. What impresses me about the passage above is not the syllogistically framed declaration, but the way the mind dwells, almost lovingly, on the (theoretically) unreal particulars: the plate, the bread, the knife, the drink, the woman. These exist only in the mind, the poet says, and yet one wonders about his focusing on the things themselves.

Actually, Stevens' philosophical subjectivism was always open to basic qualification, and even basic questioning, for he was never quite sure of the desirability of such a position given his naturalistic orientation, or the human condition he sees in, say, "Sunday Morning." Stevens is convinced in that poem that this world of process is the best possible world. As he expressed it in his notebook, "The most beautiful thing in the world is, of course, the world itself. This is so not only logically but categorically." [10] Or, in the essay "The Figure of the Youth as Virile Poet": "Kant says that the objects of perception are conditioned by the nature of the mind as to their form. But the poet says that, whatever it may be, *la vie est plus belle que les idées.*" [11]

Why should she give her bounty to the dead?

. . . .

Shall she not find in comforts of the sun,
In pungent fruit and bright, green wings, or else
In any balm or beauty of the earth,
Things to be cherished like the thought of heaven? [12]

If we must "chant" "boisterous devotion" to this "old chaos of the sun," as he put it in the concluding stanzas of "Sunday Morning," if this life is all there is, then we ought to know exactly what that "beautiful thing" (the world of change) is like, independent of its "unreal" existence in the mind. Implicitly, at this point, an unresolvable dialectic shapes up in Stevens which might be schematized in this way: thesis, a world "objectively" real—categorically beautiful—from which the poet draws his *materia poetica;* antithesis, a world that has no existence except in the mind, and may or may not be beautiful, depending on how the self happens to feel about it. No matter which end of the dialectic he chooses to opt for in a particular poem, the very fact that he is aware of the dualistic nature of his experience will generate the conflict and tension of being caught in between. If the world of "Sunday Morning" is the ultimate good, then surely he ought to enjoy that world itself, not his idea of it, but he cannot get at the thing itself since it exists only in his apprehension. The poet, in apprehending the world, necessarily changes the world by enclosing it in his own subjectivity: "Things as they are / Are changed upon the blue guitar." [13]

The heavy emphasis on the world of change in "Sunday Morning" suggests an obvious variant of the basic dualism: thesis, the naturalistic world is the ultimate good; antithesis, the naturalistic world leaves a great deal to be desired. That is why the poet prefers the subjective blue glasses of the imagination: because, deep down, he is motivated to perceive beyond this world—he is not really satisfied with it—and penetrate to a realm of permanence, the logical antithesis to the world of change. The quest for permanence is ordinarily the trait of the romantic, not of the skeptical materialist. But this is what Stevens wrote in a later poem:

He wanted his heart to stop beating and his mind
    to rest

In a permanent realization, without any wild
    ducks
Or mountains that were not mountains, just to
    know how it would be,
Just to know how it would feel, released from destruction . . .

Without the oscillations of planetary pass-pass,
Breathing his bronze breath at the azury centre
    of time.[14]

"Sunday Morning" has usually been read as a poem in praise of flux and death, and, as such, Stevens' bravest and truest effort. There is evidence, however, even in "Sunday Morning," which suggests that he is not as satisfied with chaos as he seems to be:

> We live in an old chaos of the sun
> Or old dependency of day and night,
> Or island solitude, unsponsored, free,
> Of that wide water, inescapable.[15]

Why does Stevens speak of the world of "Sunday Morning" as "inescapable" when he takes such rhetorical pains to prove to us that since "Death is the mother of beauty," the yearning for permanence is futile? I would say that characteristically Stevens in his most brutally honest moments is genuinely ironic or "impure" toward any total view of reality. He would like to have, sometimes, exactly what he knows in theory he cannot have—release from destruction, permanence.

For too long critics have given "Sunday Morning" a controlling hold on Stevens' mind. As Yvor Winters wrote years ago, it is one of the most enchanting poems in English literature, but its bravura in the face of death and a posttranscendental world is not the whole Stevens by any means. Even within *Harmonium*, the volume in which "Sunday Morning" appeared, radically different feelings and attitudes toward the world emerge. No happy naturalist, no hedonist, wrote "Domination of Black" or "Anecdote of the Prince of Peacocks"; reality can be "berserk," evil, and the self retreats, at such moments, into the subjective realms of imagination:

> I knew the dread of the bushy plain,
> And the beauty of the moonlight
> Falling there,
> Falling
> As sleep falls
> In the innocent air.[16]

154

In the poignant poems of *The Rock*, written in his last years, Stevens describes a reality so barren and boring that the confident voice of "Sunday Morning" sounds like whistling in the dark:

It makes so little difference, at so much more
Than seventy, where one looks, one has been
    there before.[17]

"Sunday Morning" is not archetypal Stevens: it is a poem he wrote when the world seemed good, when earth seemed paradise enough. But when life is punctuated by the "terrible incantations of defeats," one requires "moon-mash" or poems.[18] One says at such moments, when life itself is not the source of happiness, that "Life consists / Of propositions about life." Then, the poetic proposition, as it blunts the jagged edges of experience in metaphor, will make life bearable. But, true to his dialectical frame of reference, "thought is false happiness." [19] The poetic process is, as he suggested, a never-ending meditation. And it must be because there is no way out of the dialectic, the fundamental contradictions of existential life. Stevens' poetry is the poetry of a man who feels what he perceives: when life is good, the imaginative realms are false and one does not want or need to be a subjectivist. But when life is bad, the imagination is the last refuge, and the imaginative reality of poems is the world we prefer.

"The Snow Man," [20] another early poem, is a witty treatment of the imagination–reality dialectic. "One must have a mind of winter" (consciousness must be made congruent with external reality), Stevens writes, in order to "regard" and "behold"—his verbs imply seeing and knowing—the "junipers shagged with ice." The poem is in one sentence and his rhetoric is persuasive enough to make the initial proposition attractive. But the last two lines shift the focus radically. "For the listener, who listens in the snow," who opens himself completely to the impact of external reality by dissolving, somehow, the human perspective itself, "beholds / Nothing that is not there," and thus is "nothing himself." What is the poet's choice? Stevens suggests on the one hand that by approaching nature passively, by refusing to commit the pathetic fallacy, we will not hear the sound of misery in the wind for the simple reason that reality is inhuman. Yet insofar as we do not imagine—his conclusion is not without humor—we do not exist, we are "nothing." Stevens explores the dialectic in many poems, but rarely resolves it.

Finally, "The Snow Man" stands as a hypothesis and not a possibility. In the later work Stevens increasingly insists that man apprehends his world dynamically, that the objects of perception *are* conditioned by the mind. There is a world of objects outside perception, he believed, but the eye's plain view is a version, not reality in itself. The disparity between reality itself and our perception of it would hardly seem to be capable of moving poetic treatment, but here it is in "An Ordinary Evening in New Haven":

> Inescapable romance, inescapable choice
> Of dreams, disillusion as the last illusion,
> Reality as a thing seen by the mind,
> Not that which is, but that which is apprehended,
> A mirror, a lake of reflections in a room . . .[21]

The modernist's last-ditch "romance" is played out when, in apprehension, the mirror of the mind distorts the world "out there" and we therefore do not see "that which is." But the mirror metaphor is complicated by the syntax. As R. P. Blackmur pointed out some thirty years ago, Stevens is often intentionally ambiguous at the most crucial points in his poems.[22] This is one such point, for the mirror may also be read as a figure of reality. Now, seen in this way, Stevens would be suggesting that the "inescapable romance" is not merely an unavoidable perceptual distortion, but narcissism as Allen Tate described it: reality is a reflection of the self, and the world that we know, to push to the solipsistic conclusion, does not exist outside our awareness. This is the position that one critic attributed to the French symbolists who, in their efforts to reverse the rising tide of naturalism, brought too much enthusiasm to their reading of German idealistic philosophy.[23] Stevens knew symbolist literature and sometimes found solipsism comfortable, as in "Tea at the Palaz of Hoon," because the artificial world of Hoon is wonderfully familiar and ordered, and the poet once more is at the center of his universe. But the evidence of the poetry suggests more often than not that he found solipsism the easy way out of a bad show, and the theory of the constructive imagination simply invalid: "I found between moon-rising and moon-setting / The world was round. But not from my begetting."[24]

Yet the implications of subjectivism and narcissism remain attractive for the poet raging for order in a world of chaos. One of Stevens' finest considerations of the idea is "Le Monocle de Mon Oncle." In the beautiful third stanza of "Le Monocle" he looks at the poets who create value and order from within the self:

> Is it for nothing, then, that old Chinese
> Sat tittivating by their mountain pools
> Or in the Yangtse studied out their beards?
> I shall not play the flat historic scale.
> You know how Utamaro's beauties sought
> The end of love in their all-speaking braids. . . .
> Alas! Have all the barbers lived in vain
> That not one curl in nature has survived?[25]

The poets, or as Stevens figures them, the barbers, have lived in vain because the myths with which they ordered reality ("curls") derived no vitality from history, but originated wholly in the dying, finite self: they studied out their beards in reality's "pool," the "powerful mirror of . . . wish and will."[26] All such mythologizing, though in some sense inevitable—since poets are in love with their own imaginations, the "interior paramour" [27]—is finally futile because

It is the human that is the alien,
The human that has no cousin in the moon.

It is the human that demands his speech
From beasts or from the incommunicable mass.[28]
Myths are static orders and suit well the tailor-made reality of the solipsist, but since Stevens does not really doubt the external world, he can write: "It is a wheel, the rays / Around the sun. The wheel survives the myths." [29] The "permanent" worlds created by the imagination are necessary because they satisfy a basic human need for order, but not for long because they are fictions.

Far from being a doctrinal solipsist, Stevens (in his aesthetic) claims that there is an objective reality, and that the poet can and must draw on it for his *materia poetica*. The aphorisms collected under the title *Adagia* express the idea: "The real is only the base. But it is the base"; "The imagination must not detach itself from reality"; "All our ideas come from the natural world." These statements imply a kind of common-sense, realistic epistemology which contradicts the lines quoted from "An Ordinary Evening in New Haven." Stevens is not suggesting that the poet's function, in the final analysis, is to be a secretary to the world of fact (as Balzac would have it), nor is he confused. Like Yeats, he found himself strung between two worlds—his dialectic—and his own ambivalent attitudes toward them. Yeats quested for permanence (figured as Byzantium), but he longed for the country of fish, flesh, and fowl, too. Stevens, translating these worlds into theoretical terms, needed the life of the imagination so that in his mediations he could compose and pattern the world as he wished, especially at those moments when the world's chaos impinged upon his sanity. The imagination is thus celebrated in "Tea at the Palaz of Hoon" and "Another Weeping Woman"

as being "the one reality / In this imagined world," but
that same faculty is treated equivocally in the passages
I quoted from "Le Monocle" and "Less and Less Human, O Savage Spirit," for being essentially false to
reality. Stevens' central attitude toward imaginative
perception is a dual one, and a typical expression of it is
in "The Ordinary Women":

Then from their poverty they rose,
From dry catarrhs, and to guitars
They flitted
Through the palace walls.

They flung monotony behind . . .[30]

The women leave reality ("their poverty," "dry catarrhs") and enter the world of imagination, figured by
the guitar, where they escape monotonous change.
This is the substance of the first stanza. The last stanza
reads:

Then from their poverty they rose,
From dry guitars, and to catarrhs
They flitted
Through the palace walls.[31]

By juxtaposing "guitars" and "catarrahs" (almost homo-
nyms), Stevens compresses meaning, epitomizes his
dialectical and ironic structure, and implies that there is
something basically dissatisfying and sterile about permanence (the imaginative world) as well as change
(the naturalistic world). In "Sunday Morning" materialistic reality is the ultimate good; in "Arrival at
the Waldorf" poetry and the imagination are called
wild rhapsodic fakes, northern substitutes for reality,
evoked as "point-blank, green and actual Guatemala."
But elsewhere, in "Gubbinal" for example, "The world
is ugly / And the people are sad" because the lush,
green world is also the inhuman world of process, the
world of pain, and of the poor old woman who, in the
first section of *Owl's Clover*, destroys man's imaginative creations by her mere presence.

Finally, neither Yeats nor Stevens could be fully satisfied with either the imaginative or the real world, nor could they maintain a static attitude toward either half of the antinomy. Some of their best poems suggest that the mind can never be satisfied, as Stevens put it; that wanting it both ways at once they were doomed to perpetual discontent. Again, in "An Ordinary Evening" we find this uneasy mixture of tone:

> We keep coming back and coming back
> To the real: to the hotel instead of the hymns
> That fall upon it out of the wind. We seek
>
> The poem of pure reality, untouched
> By trope or deviation, straight to the word,
> Straight to the transfixing object, to the object
>
> At the exactest point at which it is itself. . . .[32]

In its repetitions and refinements the passage is characteristic of the later Stevens. Here the repetition is not a sign of shoddy writing, as it seems to be in some of the later work, but an essential feature of Stevens' method of creating a range of meaning while apparently making a flat statement. We keep coming back and coming back to reality because we keep going away and going away. Reality is imaged accurately by the "hotel"—a place we might enjoy for a few days, but not for a lifetime. For Stevens the hotel is all there is and to endure it we need its hymns (or poems). He uses the hymn to figure the poem in a number of places,[33] and I think he wants us to keep the religious context in mind. A hymn that is a song of reality would, for the believer, probably include a resolution of life in time to timeless transcendental life. The hymn would be partly about this world (the hotel), but finally about the other world. Because for Stevens the hotel is a "mangled, smutted semi-world hacked out / of dirt," [34] and because it has no transcendental completion, the hymn becomes the glorious self-delusion of the imagination. From this perspective, the absolutely true poem would be the "poem of pure reality," untouched by the language of hymns which in the vision of the naturalist is an evasion of reality. Stevens extends his metaphor further and then makes the ironic contradiction that creates the tone of irresolution:

> We seek
> Nothing beyond reality. Within it
> Everything, the spirit's alchemicana
> Included, the spirit that goes roundabout
> And through included, not merely the visible,
> The solid, but the movable, the moment,
> The coming on of feasts, and the habits of saints,
> The pattern of the heavens and high, night air.[35]

Spirit in Stevens is not soul but imagination, and his hymns are not the poetry of the soul in praise of God and paradise, but constructions of the imagination. Religious hymns and secular poems alike, however, are "alchemicana," the would-be magical formulations of a "sensibility in desperation,"[36] a sensibility that requires more than the given world of brute fact but cannot in all honesty say that incantation or alchemy actually facilitates any traditionally religious or occultist transcendence. In his naturalistic mood, Stevens believes that the poem should only be "a part of the res itself," and not about it, a slice of pure reality and not a falsifying hymn; he believes this in his coldly theoretical moments but he requires more than that—apparently the "res" is not enough—and frankly says so: "We seek / Nothing beyond reality. Within it, / Everything, the spirit's alchemicana / Included." While the factive, "no" voice of Stevens demands that the poem be fully anchored in the real world, the impossible-to-repress "yes" voice demands transcendence: "the spirit that goes roundabout / And through included."

The impossibility of achieving cognitive certainty of the beyond (which may not even exist) through imaginative perception leaves Stevens with two alternatives: (1) he might try to see everything within a chaotic material universe, including the aesthetic orderings of the imagination; or he might consider even the orderings of the imagination to be desperate constructions of the will in search of adequacy and (2) seek the poem of flux itself. These oppositions generate one of the basic themes of *Notes toward a Supreme Fiction*. The opening poem of *Notes* is crucial because it deals with first principles in the dialectical, ironic mode. Assuming the role of the master, Stevens addresses the "ephebe," a young man entering upon his poetic maturity:

> Begin, ephebe, by perceiving the idea
> Of this invention, this invented world,
> The inconceivable idea of the sun.
>
> You must become an ignorant man again
> And see the sun again with an ignorant eye
> And see it clearly in the idea of it.[37]

The sun is Stevens' emblem for material reality, and its "idea," its transcendent informing principle, is at the least "inconceivable," beyond man's knowledge, and probably nonexistent, as he suggested in another poem.[38] But reality can be perceived, and in perception we integrate the chaos of nature and in effect "invent" reality, as Stevens puts it. Beneath the first six lines lies a variation on Stevens' familiar antinomy: the world as we know it and change it in percepion ("that which is apprehended"), and the world outside perception, the world of inhuman chaos in itself, whose independent existence he accepts on naturalistic faith. The confrontation of imagination and reality, Stevens' great theme, cannot issue in coherent reciprocity of mind and matter as it can, theoretically, for a romantic idealist, because the two worlds (mind and matter) exist in a dualism, not in a preestablished harmony.

162

There can be no organic interpenetration of the imagination (a human faculty) and reality, because the cry of the ocean or the cry of the leaves is an inhuman cry concerning no one at all, as he put it in a late poem. Or, in the words of the famous anthology piece, "The Idea of Order at Key West," "the water never formed to mind or voice." Any "relationship" of imagination and reality is thus a forced, unnatural one.

Yet, in spite of the discrepancy and incoherence he postulates between the perceived world and the objective world, Stevens continues to admonish his young student (and perhaps confuse him, too, as only an ironic teacher could) to see the sun in its idea, to penetrate to the thing itself, because such a perception, somewhat illogically, would be the basis of a new poetic peculiarly suited to Darwin's reality of process, and not to Plato's reality of fixed ideas. Stevens was fond of saying that the poetic theory and mythology of the twentieth century must be based on the fact of flux itself. Already, however, we have seen this idea countered ironically in "An Ordinary Evening in New Haven" when he wrote of the "poem of pure reality." But some of his critics have taken his words at face value and have speculated that what he actually meant was that the poem of pure reality would be based on the idea or source of transformation and process. This, I believe, is making him a transcendentalist of some sort. He considers the very issue in a late poem aptly called "Human Arrangement," but his conclusion is strongly ambivalent: ". . . the centre of transformations that / Transform for transformation's self" is a projection of the imagination toward which Stevens expresses his double attitude: it is "true-unreal," "true" in the sense that desire makes it so, but "unreal" because he knows that what the imagination makes is simply not demonstrably true.[39] In the first poem of *Notes* he considers the issue again:

How clean the sun when seen in its idea
Washed in the remotest cleanliness of a heaven
That has expelled us and our images. . . .[40]

Since Stevens has but a few lines before given us a
subjectivist position, this passage can be taken only as
nostalgic desire: the self and its images can never be
totally expelled from reality, though one may avoid
blind solipsism. He continues to speak to the ephebe,
however, as if he were utterly rational about the matter, and orates like the sophomore who has just discovered that God does not exist and is determined to tell
the world:

The death of one god is the death of all.
Let purple Phoebus lie in umber harvest,
Let Phoebus slumber and die in autumn umber,

Phoebus is dead, ephebe. But Phoebus was
A name for something that never could be
    named. . . .[41]

Then, as if catching the false bravado in his own dogmatic voice, Stevens punctures his doctrine and in a
sense forewarns his reader not to take him too seriously when he waxes philosophic. By writing, paradoxically, "The sun must bear no name, gold flourisher,"
he admits that we must name, that we must fix reality
in a metaphor, even though metaphorical orders are
false to the nature of things.[42] Incapable of discovering significance in the "meaningless plungings of water
and wind," [43] the self wills significance through the
imagination, but such significance is only fictional, and
only momentarily satisfying.[44]

The distinctions and ironies underlying the opening
poem of Notes give us a basis for interpreting the
climactic and often disputed final poems ("It Must
Give Pleasure," v–x). Harold Bloom's point of view [45]
summarizes the attitudes of many recent commenta-
tors. According to Bloom, Notes brings to a climax the
whole tradition of romantic poetry not only by achiev-

ing the "marriage of imagination and reality," but also by presenting a discovery of order in imaginative apprehension. But there can be no true Coleridgean marriage of imagination and reality, as Stevens ironically indicated in his opening verses; and of the possibility of discovering order he is less than assured. Describing his alter ego Canon Asprin he writes, "He imposes orders as he thinks of them," and then, sardonically, "It is a brave affair." To impose an order is to distort reality, but this would seem to be unavoidable in the scheme of *Notes*. The ideal, objective meaning, a meaning not dependent on the self, necessitates discovering, not imposing order:

> But to impose is not
> To discover. To discover an order as of
> A season, to discover summer and know it,
> To discover winter and know it well, to find,
> Not to impose, not to have reasoned at all,
> Out of nothing to have come on major
> weather. . . .[46]

The passage is at the core of Stevens and echoes the problems I have been sketching. The resolutions usually offered were less definitive resolutions than they were ironic, qualified, sometimes desperate, sometimes comic, oppositions and alternatives. The answer in *Notes* is desperate:

> It is possible, possible, possible. It must
> Be possible. It must be that in time
> The real will from its crude compoundings
> come. . . .[47]

I find it difficult to read this passage as a confident statement bringing the tradition of romantic poetry to a climax. In the last poem of *Notes* Stevens addresses reality as his "Fat Girl," saying with characteristic doubleness, "You are familiar yet an aberration." Accepting the human limitations and needs that he himself often took pains to define, and no longer stridently declaring "It is possible," he writes:

Civil madam, I am, but underneath
A tree, this improved sensation requires

That I should name you flatly, waste no words,
Check your evasions . . .[48]

The idea of "unresolved dialectic" is, I believe, a
fairly accurate way of describing the defining form and
tension of Stevens' poems. Whitman has also been described this way. A comparison may be instructive if
we note that in Stevens the opposed images, values,
and attitudes are not prophetically synthesized in suggested intuitions of cosmic harmony. Unlike Whitman,
Stevens sees the confrontation of the poetic imagination and reality, of self and world, as a fundamentally
belligerent and antagonistic face-off: his basic antinomy remains unresolved. Insofar as his poems maintain
a tone of irresolution they are true to his philosophical
orientation. Some of the shorter poems in *The Rock*,
his last volume, and in *Opus Posthumous* illustrate the
divided vision he maintained to the end. In a haunting
piece entitled "Final Soliloquy of the Interior Paramour" he writes that it is "for small reason" we "think /
the world imagined is the ultimate good." And, similarly, not "God and the imagination are one," but "We
say God and the imagination are one" (italics mine).[49]
I think his subtle qualification is all important. If he
had said "God and the imagination are one" he would
have resolved the career-long tension in his poems.
We, then, would be justified in claiming that he was a
passionate humanist who no longer lusted for the transcending powers of the idealistic imagination, who felt
that the limited, finite imagination was adequate to the
needs of the modern, impoverished self. But he did
make the qualification, and in so doing generated an
image in the poem, not of a passionate humanist, but
of the man who has had humanism thrust upon him
and who knows too well the differences between what
man creates and what God might have created.

166

"The Course of a Particular," published in 1951, puts it all very sadly and unmistakably:

> Today the leaves cry, hanging on branches swept
> by wind,
> Yet the nothingness of winter becomes a little
> less.
> It is still full of icy shades and shapen snow.
>
> The leaves cry. . . . One holds off and merely
> hears the cry.
> It is a busy cry, concerning someone else.
> And though one says that one is a part of every-
> thing,
>
> There is a conflict, there is a resistance in-
> volved;
> And being part is an exertion that declines;
> One feels the life of that which gives life as it is.
>
> The leaves cry. It is not a cry of divine atten-
> tion,
> Nor the smoke-drift of puffed-out heroes, nor hu-
> man cry,
> It is the cry of leaves that do not transcend them-
> selves,
>
> In the absence of fantasia, without meaning more
> Than they are in the final finding of the ear, in
> the thing
> Itself, until, at last, the cry concerns no one at
> all.[50]

While affirming the need for coherence by making leaves cry like humans, Stevens denies the possibility of coherence. In the light of his honest uncertainties, we are not warranted in claiming too much for his doctrines of the imagination. Stevens is a humble poet who believed that though the imagination is all we have, neither it nor its creations will suffice for long.

We can create "permanent" orders with the imagination if we wish, he would say (and he did), but we must see the order so created as an imposition of the will, momentary self-delusion, and not a discovery of something more deeply interfused.

METAPHOR AND THE CONSTRUCTIVE IMAGINATION

"The Idea of Order at Key West" is probably Wallace Stevens' most famous poem. It is not difficult to understand why: first of all it deals quite directly with his master themes; second, it is not nearly so difficult as *Notes*, "The Comedian as the Letter C," or "The Man with the Blue Guitar," a quality that has endeared the poem to many who want to get a grip on Stevens' doctrines; and finally, it appears to summarize the "problem" of the modern poet and offer, in a well-known passage, a solution to that problem and, even more, a *raison d'être* for art in a century that has seen it come under the attack of those logical positivists who arrogantly demean the role of poetry in modern culture. In short, "The Idea of Order at Key West" has been made pivotal in the Stevens' canon by almost all his critics, and pivotal to the fate of modern literature by his enthusiasts. I find it easy to agree with his critics (though not always for the same reasons), but not with his enthusiasts, who, I believe, mistakenly see him at the forefront of the powerful thrust of the neo-Kantian tradition in aesthetics, wherein the poetic imagination and the poem are seen as autotelic modes of perception and expression. This is the main thrust of modern theoretical discussion, but it is not Wallace Stevens.

In the first part of this chapter I tried to show that Stevens' poetry, unlike his prose, does not lend itself to systematic doctrinal interpretation because it is as much a poetry of irrational feeling as it is a poetry of

168

thought. In this section I suggest the centrality of "Key West" by outlining its context through an analysis of what appears to be a group of related poems. What Stevens says in "Key West" about the constructive imagination ("She was the single artificer of the world") seems prescriptive of his own theory and practice. He seems to be putting himself firmly into the nineteenth-century traditions of symbolism. I say "seems" because I do not believe that he is really doing so. I think my point will be substantiated by an explication of the full text, and not just certain selected passages. Therefore, I shall close this chapter by examining in some detail "The Idea of Order at Key West," in the hope that such an examination, when placed in its proper context, will offer a statement of the relationship of Stevens' poems to the theoretical traditions I sketched in the second chapter. First, however, some of his considerations of metaphor and the constructive imagination.

Stevens' characteristic poetic tone is mixed: often he feels impelled to make a grandiose statement on imagination behind which he can stand as the man who established the ontological and cognitive significance of art in a world shorn of idealistic systems of form and value, a world in which scientific method is the only way of finding truth, and imaginative apprehension and activity is merely make-believe. From one perspective, then, he looks as if he were standing on the shoulders of Kant, Mallarmé, and T. E. Hulme. Contrarily, however, we saw how he tended to agree with the naturalists by undercutting all of his grand doctrine as fanciful self-delusion. The real Stevens, I believe, feels both motivations. One of the finest, but not so well-known, *Harmonium* poems entitled "Negation" very neatly expresses this duality:

Hi! The creator too is blind,
Struggling toward his harmonious whole,
Rejecting intermediate parts,

169

Horrors and falsities and wrong;
Incapable-master of all force,
Too vague idealist, overwhelmed
By an afflatus that persists.
For this, then, we endure brief lives,
The evanescent symmetries
From that meticulous potter's thumb.[51]

Stevens is speaking of the artist and what the artist can do with the imaginative faculty. The poem will not bear very much speculation. It is impossible to say, definitively, that Stevens has a symbolist view of art specifically in mind. We can say, however, that he is writing about a constructor, a maker of an aesthetic, and (if a poet specifically) a verbal universe. What counts is Stevens' attitude toward the maker and his aesthetic world. The essential attitude, the exact tone, seems to lie in the poem's dialectical tensions. The opening line—"Hi! The creator too is blind"—is flippant and comic, and Stevens' oxymoronic characterization of the maker as an "Incapable-master"—who in making his world rejects all that resists the informing poetic spirit—is mocking. That much is clear, but it is only half of the poem. For it is also clear that the poem generates a certain amount of seriousness and genuine pathos: "For this, then, we endure brief lives." Stevens suggests that the artist and the aesthetic object may be inadequate in a confrontation with the whole of reality in all its rawness; poetry may be, finally, a "finikin thing of air," but nevertheless it is our only weapon, our only comfort, and it "lasts beyond much lustier blurs." [52]

A similar duality of feeling toward the constructive imagination emerges in the much-anthologized and disputed "Anecdote of the Jar." The jar, a figure for the imagination, "took dominion" over reality (Tennessee). But in its very act of dominance the jar distorts reality; it evades the hard particulars of nature, or, if it does not evade them, it is at least incapable of producing them: "It did not give of bird or bush / Like noth-

170

ing else in Tennessee." Like "Negation" the poem offers unresolved and disparate attitudes. The imagination either makes a verbal cosmos—a symbolist and contextualist ideal—or it imposes its own order on reality. But in either event, the imagination is incapable of truly coming to grips with reality. And Stevens knows it. The conjunction of imagination and reality, when there is conjunction and not plain evasion, is uneasy and unnatural, not organic. The symbolist side of the doctrine is its "bright" side, the side that many recent apologists for art would stress. But Stevens saw the darker aspects, those that make the imagination a tool of the self's need for order ("evanescent symmetries"), a need so great that it will be satisfied even in distortion and fakery.

Now I should like to extend this discussion of the imagination by considering "Of Modern Poetry," a poem often alluded to by those critics who feel that it defines Stevens' basic view of the creative process against the backdrop of a naturalistic world. "Of Modern Poetry" begins:

> The poem of the mind in the act of finding
> What will suffice. It has not always had
> To find: the scene was set; it repeated what
> Was in the script.
> Then the theatre was changed
> To something else. Its past was a souvenir.[53]

It is the "act of finding" that defines existential man as artist, not the thing found, because the thing found inevitably passes away in the flux of history. Poets in the past had a "permanent" theater and a script; the romantics, the most obvious illustration, created in Schelling's idealistic universe in which the perceiving self and reality were spiritually coherent: the subject-object distinction was dissolved. This was their theater. Their script, to continue in terms of the metaphor of a self and a world mutually interpenetrative, was either "objective" nature or the "subjective" ego; both scripts were identical, both scripts told of the unity and parity of beauty, truth, and goodness. The poem written according to the script was a window to those values. The romantic poet opted for permanence—an eternally vital poem windowing an eternally deified universe—but time, Darwin, and the naturalists seemed to upset all that; the romantic theater was relegated to the junk heap—for the sentimentalists, the antique store.

The modern poem, for Stevens, must rest on a theoretical foundation that owes much to the philosophical naturalism that helped to bury romanticism in its pristine form. It will be a poem of process itself; it will be made of the particulars (the pleasant and the horrible) of modern experience; the modern poem will mirror Darwin's reality:

> It has to be living, to learn the speech of the place.
> It has to face the men of the time and to meet
> The women of the time. It has to think about war . . .[54]

Such a poem, which will adhere to the truth of a particular contemporary scene, will like the scene itself be transient: the men and women of the scene live and die; wars come and go; speech, as linguistic scholars tell us, is in a state of continual change. As Joseph Riddel notices, such a poem soon becomes stale, and the imagination is forced continually to re-create according to the dictates of a changing reality.[55] Ideally, there will always be a new confrontation of poet and reality and the creative process itself will be *in process*. But what Riddel fails to notice is that Stevens, like his romantic forebears, wants a theater of his own which will at least seem to offer a world of permanence or stasis:

> It has
> To construct a new stage. It has to be on that stage
> And, like an insatiable actor, slowly and

172

With meditation, speak words in the ear,
In the delicatest ear of the mind, repeat
Exactly, that which it wants to hear . . .[56]

The image that emerges is both grotesque and ironic.
The modern "poem of the mind" has suddenly stopped
its act of finding; has, in fact, abstracted from the particulars and constructed a "stage," a world. And on
that stage it stands, the modern poem, like a vain and
pompous actor, narcissistically gorging himself on all
the brilliant lines he can concoct, talking them somehow into his own ear. The poem has moved to the position that it implicitly rejects in its opening lines. The
quest for a poem based on naturalistic assumptions,
rooted in Darwin's reality, has turned in on itself and
we are back where we started, but with a difference:
the new romantic script has no idealistic framework,
only a huge egoistic motivation: the poem of the mind
in the act of finding becomes the poem of the mind in
the act of looking at itself and pronouncing the image
good. We have come full circle and are looking once
again at that third stanza of "Le Monocle de Mon
Oncle." [57] Like the old Chinese, Stevens sometimes
studies his beard in reality's pool.

In form and intent, "Of Modern Poetry" resembles
"Negation" and "Anecdote of the Jar." The meaning of
the three poems lies in the exquisite dialectical tension
created by Stevens' unresolved attitudes toward the
imagination. In "Negation" and "Anecdote of the Jar"
the imagination is seen by the ironist as being untrue
to reality in the very process of making its own cosmos. In "Of Modern Poetry" the imagination (or, better, the poet's will) is seen as unavoidably distorting
reality because of its inherent propensity to establish a
world beyond change. And yet, the ironic self, strong
as it is in these pieces, does not nullify the lyric self
that quests for permanence and could not care less
about "truth."

One may still insist on viewing Stevens through the

eyes of the symbolists. But if we look at the poems carefully, I think we see that he simply does not believe in the theory that the poetic imagination gives access to a unique realm of knowledge. Especially in the three shorter poems I have just discussed, and in many of the passages I examined in the first section of this chapter, we catch Stevens with a tongue-in-cheek posture when writing about the creator of a so-called permanent aesthetic universe. The law of material reality is the law of change; Stevens would also make it the law of poetry. But at the same time his imagination, impelled by desire, seeks permanence in its fictions—his central paradox. The quest for permanence, however, does not get his intellectual allegiance. For him, poems can hope to be significant only insofar as they remain faithful to his idea of the structure of reality, and that structure is fluid. Whenever the poet, seeking what will suffice, attempts to mitigate chaos by creating coherence within the mind, without realizing that coherence is a fabricated illusion of his desperate will, then the creator is blind, and the poem represents a dishonest evasion of reality.

Before reading very far into *Harmonium*, we come across a strange poem called "Metaphors of a Magnifico." Yvor Winters found the poem strange, too, and called it "willful nonsense." [58] If it is looked at as anything but ironic play, Winters is right. Seen, however, as a wry statement on the limitations of metaphor the poem presents little difficulty. Stevens begins by trying to discover through metaphor an underlying unity in reality:

> Twenty men crossing a bridge,
> Into a village,
> Are twenty men crossing twenty bridges,
> Into twenty villages,
> Or one man
> Crossing a single bridge into a village. [59]

Metaphors are alogical, symbolists tell us; but they are, in their very alogicality, exposing relationships, discovering aspects of the real which scientific language can never account for. In a modern extension of Kant's thinking, Philip Wheelwright has made metaphor itself uniquely constitutive of certain otherwise hidden aspects of being.[60] Stevens does not believe it. His attempt at such a conception of metaphor is dismissed as an insoluble puzzle: "This is old Song / That will not declare itself." In so many words he calls his metaphors cognitively meaningless, and he begins again:

> Twenty men crossing a bridge,
> Into a village,
> Are
> Twenty men crossing a bridge
> Into a village.[61]

The comic element is introduced with the tautology, and Stevens follows it with a witty commentary:

> That will not declare itself
> Yet is certain as meaning . . .

Again he begins, in a search for meaning, and this time very tortuously. But he punctures his thought with "of what was it I was thinking? / So the meaning escapes." The poem ends with no statement of "metaphysical" meaning, but with a bare image, a perception: "The first white wall of the village . . . / The fruit trees . . ." The moral of the story seems to be that though the image yields only itself, the metaphor yields even less.

The broad import of "Metaphors of a Magnifico" is that Stevens does not hold that metaphor is a valid way of understanding reality. The regularity with which he addressed himself to the problem, and the consistency of his conclusions, indicate that the voice of "Metaphors of a Magnifico" is that of Stevens himself. In "Add This to Rhetoric," for example, metaphor is again evasion and distortion, but it is something more, besides:

> In the way you speak
> You arrange, the thing is posed,

What in nature merely grows.
Tomorrow when the sun,
For all your images,
Comes up as the sun, bull fire,
Your images will have left
No shadow of themselves.[62]

Here Stevens is agreeing with the logical positivist, saying, in effect, that poetic language fixes and arranges nature in a way that it never could be. Poetic structures are unnatural (they leave no shadows in the sun); they are merely illusions which have no status in being. But in the very act of denying the ontological value of poetry, Stevens affirms the psychological necessity of poeticizing and fixing the experience of inhuman reality (the sun) in humanistic terms —hence the metaphor "bull fire."

Behind his skeptical view of metaphor lies a conception of reality which differentiates Stevens sharply from the romantic traditions, and reemphasizes the impact of naturalistic thought upon his aesthetic. The cold, inhuman nature of Darwin and Marx is the context of poetry for Stevens. Nature was the context of poetry for Emerson, too; Stevens, however, does not see words as signs of natural facts, and natural facts as symbolic of spiritual reality. His universe is not structured as idealistic philosophy structured Emerson's. The modern imagination and nature are not organically interpenetrative as they were in romantic faith, but, rather, drastically incoherent: man not only lives in a world he never made, but in a world so different from himself that he can have no true intercourse with it. But the imaginative self, though not continuous with nature, yet imposes its constructs on the natural world by animating the inhuman reality in analogy. A passage from a poem published late in Stevens' career indicates the continuity of his thought with regard to metaphor:

. . . to speak of the whole world as metaphor
Is still to stick to the contents of the mind

And the desire to believe in a metaphor.
It is to stick to the nicer knowledge of
Belief, that what it believes in is not true.[63]
Stevens' attitudes toward metaphor are finally quite similar to his attitudes toward the imagination, constructive or otherwise. One would like to believe that one penetrates to another world in aesthetic perception; one would like to believe in permanence imaginatively constructed; one would like to believe that metaphor saliently links self and nature in a deeper harmony; one would like to believe all these propositions because one is human and desires so much more than is possible—but, Stevens knows, all the beliefs are untrue *even though he goes on making metaphors:*

It is a wheel, the rays
Around the sun. The wheel survives the myths.
And yet, in the very next line, "The *fire eye* in the clouds . . ." Stevens suggested many times that the ultimate value is reality. We can see how much he meant it. Reality is characterized by change and language tends to fix reality, and so falsify it: this is the ground of his irony toward the techniques of his craft, but the irony is evidence, too, that he persisted in making metaphors, that his desire often outran his poetic.

The last poem on the subject of metaphor I wish to consider is "The Motive for Metaphor"; while implicitly making the same criticism of the language of poetry his other poems made, it offers the reason for metaphor. The cleavage between the metaphorical creation of resemblance (the making of a "fiction") and unabstracted reality (truth), when looked at from the perspective of the impoverished self, becomes a good thing. Stevens centers his imagery upon autumn and spring, seasons symbolic of change in a world of change, and parallels the comforts of spring to the comforts of metaphor: one likes spring because it is somehow unreal in its lack of stark definition, which is not true of summer in Stevens' schema. For similar reasons one likes metaphor: through it we can blunt the starkness of reality at will. We fictionalize experience so that we may endure it:

> You like it under the trees in autumn,
> Because everything is half dead.
> The wind moves like a cripple among the leaves
> And repeats words without meaning.
>
> In the same way you were happy in spring,
> With the half colors of quarter-things,
> The slightly brighter sky, the melting clouds,
> The single bird, the obscure moon—
>
> The obscure moon lighting an obscure world
> Of things that would never be quite expressed,
> Where you yourself were never quite yourself
> And did not want nor have to be,
>
> Desiring the exhilarations of changes:
> The motive for metaphor, shrinking from
> The weight of primary noon,
> The A B C of being,
>
> The ruddy temper, the hammer
> Of red and blue, the hard sound—
> Steel against intimation—the sharp flash,
> The vital, arrogant, fatal, dominant X.[64]

In Stevens' vocabulary "metaphor," "evasion," "metamorphosis," and "change" tend to be synonymous. We like the changes of metaphor because we do not care to face nakedly the external world of change or flow. Here I think we would agree with Eugene Nassar's idea that "It must change" (a section of *Notes*) means two things: first that the poem, like the world outside, must change, and, second, that the poem must change (or distort) the world outside. Between the self and chaos we place the poem, a fictional (or metaphoric) transformation of chaos which helps us to live our lives. The ironic Stevens warns himself, however, that the order created in metaphor is not perceived, not inherent in reality, but a willed illusion of the imagination.

"THE IDEA OF ORDER AT KEY WEST"

She sang beyond the genius of the sea.
The water never formed to mind or voice,
Like a body wholly body, fluttering
Its empty sleeves; and yet its mimic motion
Made constant cry, caused constantly a cry,
That was not ours although we understood,
Inhuman, of the veritable ocean.[65]

A frequently anthologized poem, "The Idea of Order at Key West" has generally been taken as straight philosophical doctrine, and most critics cite these well-known lines,

She was the single artificer of the world
In which she sang. And when she sang, the sea,
Whatever self it had, became the self
That was her song, for she was the maker,

as its substance. But there is much more to the poem than that, and I would suggest that this often-quoted passage on imagination, when read in context, does not support the claims of the poem's critics. The poem is essentially about the confrontation of the poetic imagination and modern reality, and the imagination's function within that reality. But what is Stevens saying about reality? It is my position that "The Idea of Order at Key West" is painfully ambivalent, that Stevens evokes in the poem something like the antithesis to the harmonious self–reality relationship postulated in romantic thought. A number of critics, including Frank Kermode and Marius Bewley, see a Coleridgean doctrine of the imagination postulated in "Key West." [66] But Coleridge theorized about a *coequal* interpenetration of imagination and nature, a spiritually vitalized universe as well as a poetic mind that could shape reality.[67] Stevens' attitudes are rooted in neither postulate.

The opening lines of "Key West" (my epigraph) are difficult because they are a condensation of Stevens' ambiguous feelings about his imagination–reality dialectic. The first line suggests the confrontation of singer and sea, his constant emblems for the artist and reality. Why, we might ask, does she sing *beyond* the "genius" of reality? Why does Stevens speak of a "genius," which in the classical tradition signifies the ordering, tutelary, presiding god or spirit of a place? Here the place is quite simply the whole of perceived reality. Now, if reality has a genius, then reality has an inherent order. But for Stevens reality has no order, at least no order discoverable to the human intellect or imagination: "There is order in neither sea nor sun." [68] We need not, however, go outside the poem to see that "genius" is ironic because later in the poem Stevens offers his consistent view of that inscrutable reality of "meaningless plungings of water and the wind." The old view of an objectively, divinely ordered reality is forevermore invalid.

"The water never formed to mind or voice." The poetic imagination and reality could not interpenetrate, or coalesce, because the poetic faculty and reality are unbridgeable, separated by the gulf between like and unlike. What we have here is something like the aesthetician's version of the Cartesian crux, the dualism of subject (poet) and object (sea). This is another strike against the romantic interpretation of the poem's theoretical basis. For the romantic coherence of subject and object is rooted in Schelling's idea of a spiritually unified self–world relationship, on the idea that perceiver and perceived are "co-instantaneous," as Coleridge phrased it, or, to cite a modern romantic, Jacques Maritain, "co-natural." [69] It is thus an impossibility, epistemologically and ontologically, for the artist to sing *with* the sea. In a dualistic, incoherent universe, the poet is forced to retreat into the subjective self.

The water never formed to mind or voice,
Like a body wholly body, fluttering
Its empty sleeves . . .

Here, in Stevens' own terms, is the poetic expression of the philosophical problem. If body and mind are truly dual then they cannot interact. Likewise, mind and sea never coalesce because the sea is like a "body wholly body," a body void of "mind," "spirit," "genius," "soul," or "imagination"—pure object. But this further characterization of the sea "fluttering / Its empty sleeves" is problematic, and I gladly take the hint Arthur Mizener offered, somewhat off the cuff, in an article in the *Kenyon Review*. In his essay Mizener suggests that a ghost flutters its empty sleeves.[70] His suggestion is a cogent one because it ties in with other important aspects of this poem and other of Stevens' poems as well: "ghostlier demarcations," "pale Ramon" (has he seen a ghost?), and the "genius" of the first line which the *Oxford English Dictionary* tells us was a synonym for "ghost" or "soul" in the Middle Ages. And while we are talking about ghosts we might recall that metaphor is sometimes characterized by Stevens with the phrase "ghostly sequences / Of the mind," [71] and, moreover, that the solipsist poet who derives all order and value from within the self and toward whom Stevens is deeply ironic, is described as a "studious ghost" in "Le Monocle de Mon Oncle." Stevens has crammed into the idea of the "ghost" in many of his poems, and particularly in "Key West," a mass of ironic intent which, once perceived, clarifies his attitudes toward poetry, the poetic faculty, and the artist himself.

> . . . and yet its mimic motion
> Made constant cry, caused constantly a cry,
> That was not ours although we understood,
> Inhuman, of the veritable ocean.

The cry of the ocean is as doubly ironic as the cry of the leaves in the late poem, "The Course of a Particular." Because he sees nature as the absurd "other," man makes leaves cry just as he cries: he likes to *feel* that there is coherence, knowing that leaves do not cry.

The modern self imaged in Stevens is not involved with nature: the cry of the ocean finally concerns us not at all. Stevens' artist sang beyond the genius of the sea because the sea's genius is a ghost in the colloquial rather than the medieval sense of the word. And in singing beyond that world of chaos which she could not shape in the creative process, she neglected the real entirely. To forsake the real world by constructing one's *mundos* wholly in the imagination is a basically dishonest act in Stevens' poetic.[72]

> The sea was not a mask. No more was she.
> The song and water were not medleyed sound
> Even if what she sang was what she heard,
> Since what she sang was uttered word by word.
> It may be that in all her phrases stirred
> The grinding water and the gasping wind;
> But it was she and not the sea we heard.

Empirical nature no longer is the springboard to spirit. The sea is not a symbol of spiritual reality, just a "body wholly body." That the singer was not a symbolic mask either is Stevens' way of suggesting that the poetic self is always discrete and subjective. It is not connected to universal being (romantic idealism) nor is it a depersonalized, objective self which the symbolist poet projects in an effort to free the poem from his own psychological history. The idea that the sound of the sea and the sound of her music were not medleyed is yet another variation on "the water never formed to mind or voice," an underscoring of the alienated self. The construct of the imagination (song or poem) does not grow out of the chaos of reality, but represents, in music or in language, the deepest personal desires of the poet—the will to order. Pointed in this passage is the essential evading action of the imagination. In "Negation" the creator rejects all that displeases him; from the opposite point of view in "An Ordinary Evening in New Haven," the poem that was to be a "part of the res itself" and not about it becomes unavoidably the poem of the imagination's fanciful *mundos,* or "alchemicana." [73] Here in "The Idea of Order at Key West" the lady sings what she hears, but what she hears and what she sings are not the same thing for psychological as well as epistemological reasons: why should she sing of "chaos," which is what she would sing of if mind and sea coalesced, when it is order that she needs? The singer's imaginatively ordered aesthetic reality is what fascinates the spectators, Stevens and Fernandez, not the disordered grind of water: "But it was she and not the sea we heard."

> For she was the maker of the song she sang.
> The ever-hooded, tragic-gestured sea
> Was merely a place by which she walked to sing.
> Whose spirit is this? we said, because we knew
> It was the spirit we sought and knew
> That we should ask this often as she sang.

The incoherence of self and nature is again reemphasized—the sea was merely a place by which she walked—and the pattern of ghost-mask imagery is elaborated. The "hood" of the sea suggests the symbolic mask, which has already been denied, or even the ghost, for ghosts traditionally spook about in sheets. In Stevens' irony the ancient significations of ghost ("genius," "soul," "form") give way to the recent meaning. In the contemporary experience of reality the informing soul has been transformed into an image that haunts a child's nightmares. For beneath the hood of the sea, beneath the natural mask, lies nothing. The medieval ghost turns into a bogeyman; now, reality scares us just as the bogeyman scares a child, with the crucial difference that the bogeyman of modern reality, the ghost, is real and frightening precisely because he is not an ancient ghost (a soul), but a formless and god-deserted world. The phrase "tragic-gestured" is sadly ironic. Only the human can gesture tragically, and by making the sea do it Stevens poignantly reminds us how deep the need for coherence goes. At the same time, he gives us in "tragic-gestured" a perfect illustration of his theory of metaphor: not a discovery of what is, but a creation in language of what he would like nature to be.[74] The question that Stevens asks, then—"Whose spirit is this?"—becomes in this light not a real question but a witty one. It would be comforting to believe that the vital essence of poetry comes from the universe as well as from the poet. Not so: the spirit is the woman's, her imagination embodied in song. This is why the question was asked every time she sang:

> It was the spirit we sought and knew
> That we should ask this often as she sang.

The middle section of the poem offers more irony before revealing the identity of the "spirit." It was neither the sound of sea, sky or cloud, nor the singer's voice or the poet's interacting with nature which composed spirit ("More even than her voice, and ours, among / The meaningless plungings of water and wind"). It was her voice alone, the poetic imagination constructing an aesthetic world in which empirical reality plays little if any part at all.

> It was her voice that made
> The sky acutest at its vanishing. . . .
> She was the single artificer of the world
> In which she sang. And when she sang, the sea,
> Whatever self it had, became the self
> That was her song, for she was the maker. Then
>   we,
> As we beheld her striding there alone,
> Knew that there never was a world for her,
> Except the one she sang and, singing, made.

As I see it, the main thrust of the passage is the notion that the world she made and ordered was not the world of the sea. She failed conspicuously to do that, and she failed because she had to: the imagination can have no intercourse with reality—the sexual image of impotence is as appropriate to Stevens' poetic as the potent sexual image is for romantic theory. This is his philosophical world view, but he yet feels that the woman has become too much an escapist of the imagination, as she focuses at the horizon where the world seems to end, too willingly a solipsist who disregards the hard particulars of experience which he believes must be the ground of a vital poetry. Accordingly, he turns the full power of his irony on the singer in the penultimate section of the poem when he asks Fernandez (rhetorically), "Why, when the singing ended," did mere artifacts ("lights in the fishing boats") do what the human imagination could not do: ordered reality, however fortuitously and briefly,

> Mastered the night and portioned out the sea,
> Fixing emblazoned zones and fiery poles,
> Arranging, deepening, enchanting night.

The last section extends the irony but also points Stevens' underlying sympathy:

> Oh! Blessed rage for order, pale Ramon,
> The maker's rage to order words of the sea,
> Words of the fragrant portals, dimly-starred,
> And of ourselves and of our origins,
> In ghostlier demarcations, keener sounds.

A "rage" for order is not an achievement of order. The "rager" is desperate to order and unify reality itself ("words of the sea"), and to bring man and his world once more into the harmonious relationship that the romantics often envisioned in their moments of high faith ("and of ourselves and of our origins"). In actuality, however, the singer has rejected reality (the sea is merely a place), and created a song that is only a "ghostlier demarcation," a structure defining self and world which lacks cognitive significance. No wonder Ramon is so pale! He has seen more than one ghost: first, the ghost of reality, which, for a while, Stevens led him to believe was a "genius." Then Stevens pulled the sheet away and the ghost became, not the ordering spirit inherent in nature, but the horrible bogeyman of nature. Then he showed him the ghost of imagination which, because it did not inform reality, as the Coleridgean imagination would have, turned out to be a fake. Finally, the ghost of poetry, ideally the healer of the self-reality split, is revealed as a wholly fanciful construct of the poetic self, expressing the desperate wish for an order more deeply interfused, but yielding, in the last analysis, only a "rage for order." The rage is yet termed "blessed," however; and Stevens thereby suggests, as he always has, that no matter how pitifully inadequate the fictionalizing process might be, it is necessary therapy for a man of imagination in the twentieth century. The order of poetry is only (unfortunately) aesthetic in significance: it can not prophesy or create ontological order. (The fictive doors or "portals" of the sea open onto nothing.) But just having it is enough, sometimes, to quiet the rage.

7

Artifice as Value

". . . one writes poetry because one must."
                                                        Stevens

"This joy . . . always making and mastering."
                                                        Yeats

You were silly like us; your gift survived it all;
The parish of rich women, physical decay,
Yourself: mad Ireland hurt you into poetry.
Now Ireland has her madness and her weather still,
For poetry makes nothing happen: it survives
In the valley of its saying where executives
Would never want to tamper; it flows south
From ranches of isolation and the busy griefs,
Raw towns that we believe and die in; it survives,
A way of happening, a mouth.
                                        W. H. Auden,
                                "In Memory of W. B. Yeats"

BY INVOKING the idea of a "poetics of will" in the preceding pages, I wish to suggest both a finite imagination and a finite context for poetry which would pre-
clude idealistic, naturalistic, magical, and opaque
framing of the attitudes and theories of Yeats and Stevens. To put it positively: a poetics of will locates
poems as specific historical phenomena without denying them their special linguistic integrity. If this sounds
like a truism—that poems should function in some
unique aesthetic mode as well as play a part in the

187

larger whole we call life—then it is a truism worth repeating, because the main current of our nineteenth-century theoretical heritage could not affirm it with logical consistency.

Briefly, let me recall the conclusions of chapter 2 in which I attempted to define the critical concepts inherited from the nineteenth century. The cognitive insight assigned to the poet in romantic idealism was neither denied other men nor specifically located in the poetic context. Strictly speaking, in romantic theory a poem has no necessary historical relevance, no integral relationship to a peculiar cultural matrix, precisely because the poet exists in the continuum of spirit and nature, precisely because the poem windows that continuum—the "Absolute" that is revealed in coherent vision, the dissolution of the subject-object division. The idealistic universe does not change: the Absolute is the Absolute for all men in all places and for all time.

Naturalism, contrarily, could certainly postulate historical relevance for poetry, but not in any way substantively different from the social "sciences." "French society is the historian, I am but the secretary," wrote Balzac. A historian or a sociologist could say the same thing, probably with much more authority. Placing his faith in the philosophy and methods of later nineteenth-century science (or was it scientism?), the naturalist could not attribute unique value to the literary work.

Finally, the magical symbolist gave the imagination the power to vault over nature because, unlike the romantic idealist who worked in natural analogy, he saw nature as dead, alien matter, and not at all as spiritually coherent with the self. Such radical transcendence of the natural order forces the imagination to ignore the brute facts of history and experience. On the other hand, in its contextual anticipations, symbolist theory postulated so much special power and value for the linguistic interrelations of the poem that

188

the poem became an opaque entity that could not relate to anything but itself and still keep its unique cognitive value. When Yeats and Stevens insist, however, that poetry's primary function is not cognitive, when they suggest that a poem is neither an opaque container of nondiscursive truth nor a window to an idealistic or materialistic reality, they encourage us to conceive of poetic theory in new terms. For the metaphor of the window, though adequate to theories that affirm only one of art's two roles, cannot satisfactorily explain a poetics that encompasses both.

The poetics of will defines the imagination as a finite energy that seeks to ground itself in the linguistic medium, and isolates poems as the artifacts of the private self operating in a particular place at a particular time. The role of the poet is that of shaper or maker: the poet is not a seer or a "representative," symbolic figure; the poem is not a symbol for another reality. The continuum of nature has been fragmented. Consequently, Yeats and Stevens invite rather than discourage historical probing as they place themselves in Camus's world of "irrational bitterness," a "semi-world" with no transcendental completion. Their acceptance of the naturalistic and even existential schemes of the world of experience puts poetry irrevocably back into time. But they invite also the kind of close scrutiny of poems which one tends to associate with the contextual critic and not the literary historian.

Yeats would have sympathized with the feeling of Stevens' couplet in "Esthetique du Mal" (*Collected Poems,* p. 322):
> Natives of poverty, children of malheur,
> The gaiety of language is our seigneur.

A will is capable of holding any number of attitudes toward its world; but no matter whose will, or however complex the attitude, the poet's expression can be understood only through the poems he writes. When Stevens says that neither the self, nor nature, nor an interpene-

189

tration of the two is the storehouse of order, he leads us inexorably to his seigneur, the poem itself. For only in metaphor, in the shaping and playing with language, is the poet capable of making those illusory transformations of experience which the modern psyche requires. And, therefore, it is in the medium alone that we discover just what this particular child of malheur requires. In Stevens' view, the poem is not (in the symbolist-contextual sense) an opaque entity, but we must take it as if it were, for how else are we to know what Stevens' psyche needs, or how Stevens sees the world?

Stevens' poems are, essentially, poems of the mind's searches for what will suffice, meditative exercises touched off by the encounter of the cognitively impoverished modern imagination and an existential reality. The poem *is* order, a dike holding back the waters of chaos. But the order of the poem exists only as the aesthetic interrelations of language, and does not prophesy ultimate ontological order. The tightly woven structure of attitudes in a Stevens poem—lyric cries and rational denials—when probed, finally does reveal the world within which his poems are written. In part, the burden of chapters 5 and 6 is to portray the mind, the world from which Stevens' poems issue. But that can be accomplished only by getting inside the created contexts of the poems, and by attuning ourselves to their ironic tones. Implicitly, Stevens' theory of poetry tells us that poems cannot fulfill their double function simultaneously, but only consecutively: first the poem, the "gaiety of language," then the kind of mind and reality which the poem, once understood, finally reveals.

Yeats's emphasis is a little different. He would agree that the creative act is an assertion of freedom which a deterministic universe cannot allow. But the central catalyst of his poetry is a self encountering its world, not a desire for order—"All things are made by the struggle of the individual and the world"—and a poem, as he said often, is preeminently a thing *made*. That made self and that made world, he never tired of stressing in his mask theory, are not the natural self and the natural world, but the natural self and the natural world transformed by the artifices of poetry into something whose locus is the linguistic medium. For both Yeats and Stevens, the creative process, by being a free process, brings into the world a thing that idealistic "logic" or the "machine" of a naturalistic universe cannot generate. That thing, the poem, is at once a part of reality and a welcome release from it. Yeats's poem, "Easter 1916," though inevitably bound to a historical moment—and by design—is not simply a translation of that moment, but an addition to it, a supplementation that must be understood on its own terms before one can claim that it relates this way or that way to a particular incident.

Yeats's poems are not meditative in the sense that Stevens' are; their images tend to be drawn from the more dramatic and familiar areas of human experience as a self (as well as a mind) encounters its world. Again, however, his poetry is not an attempt to say something about a self in this world, but a "shaping joy"—Yeats's equivalent to Stevens' "gaiety of language"—the creation of a self and a world in the linguistic medium. In "Lapis Lazuli," an implicit rendering of his last poetics, Yeats leaves far behind him all cognitive theories by suggesting that, for the auditor, aesthetic value is located in the linguistic medium's power to redeem momentarily the tragic scene which it images. The tragic scene at which the two Chinamen stare is not changed by the music, just made psychologically bearable.

The impact of symbolist theory on the two poets is clear: it is not epistemological, but aesthetic in the sense that both understand a poem to be a closed system of interrelated verbal effects, whose purpose is to suggest a sense of harmony, wholeness, and unity which is not allowed by the naturalistic and existential sense of reality which they project. Even apart from the profoundly ironic tones, the rendering of the contingencies, and the exploring of antinomies, the poems exist as pieces of language forged into coherence by the poet who has had all his awesome prophetic powers stripped from him. The cognitive imagination was thrown "on the dump" when the romantic's views of reality were beat down by the naturalists. The poet who lives in Darwin's reality, not Plato's, writes poetry because he must, Stevens wrote. Yeats explained the import of Stevens' statement when he said that the poet's eye glitters as he freely and gaily makes poems, even though the poem will be beat down in time, and even though the poet's situation is irreparably and irredeemably tragic.

For the poet it is the making that counts, because (as Yeats emphasized) it is the making that launches him into an imaginative world of freedom, a world under the control of his creative will, and for the reader it is the opportunity to participate in the literary imagination by participating in the poet's created illusion. Our release and the poet's release from what Yeats called the "disordered passion of nature" and what Stevens called the "violence from without" depend upon the poet's ability to shape an ordered fictive world in the artifices of language which is not the world "out there," and on our willingness to give up the world, private and public, and to enjoy the literary cosmos for itself. Perhaps poetry serves the true, the good, the beautiful. But no matter, for the human will demands freedom from its own private agonies and those daily dealt to it by the shocks of contemporary life. With the knowledge that poetry is an "adult make-believe," as Stevens said, and with the greater knowledge that it does not matter, the mind immerses itself in the joy of the poetic medium. It is a necessity for many of us.

192

Notes

CHAPTER 1.

1 See Edmund Wilson, *Axel's Castle: A Study in the Imaginative Literature of 1870–1930* (New York, 1931); Jacques Barzun, *Classic, Romantic, and Modern* (first published 1943; Garden City, 1961); Frank Kermode, *Romantic Image* (first published 1957; New York, 1964); Richard Foster, *The New Romantics* (Bloomington, 1962).

2 See two of Harold Bloom's essays in particular: "*Notes toward a Supreme Fiction*: A Commentary," in *Wallace Stevens: A Collection of Critical Essays*, ed. Marie Borroff (Englewood Cliffs, 1963), pp. 76–95; "The Central Man: Emerson, Whitman, Wallace Stevens," *Massachusetts Review*, VII (Winter, 1966), 23–42. J. Hillis Miller's *Poets of Reality* begins with assumptions similar to my own but then follows different directions.

CHAPTER 2.

1 See, particularly, René Wellek's two articles, "The Concept of Romanticism in Literary History" and "Romanticism Re-examined," which are conveniently reprinted in his *Concepts of Criticism*, ed. and with introduction by Stephen G. Nichols, Jr. (New Haven, 1963). For readings of romanticism which inform my own see M. H. Abrams, *The Mirror and the Lamp: Romantic Theory and the Critical Tradition* (New York, 1953), esp. his third chapter, "Romantic Analogues of Art and Mind"; William K. Wimsatt, Jr., and Cleanth Brooks, *Literary Criticism: A Short History* (first published 1957; New York, 1962), esp. chaps. 18, 19; René Wellek, *A History of Modern Criticism, 1750–1950: The Romantic Age* (New Haven, 1955); Bernard Duffey, "Romantic Coherence and Romantic Incoherence in American Poetry," *Centennial Review*, VII (Spring, 1963), 219–263.

2 I have relied on Murray Krieger's brilliant treatments of contextual theory and its difficulties (*The New Apologists for Poetry* [Minneapolis, 1956]).

[3] M. H. Abrams' review of Frank Kermode's *Romantic Image* (first published 1957; New York, 1964) in *Victorian Studies*, II (Sept., 1958), 75–77. I discovered this review after my own work had been substantially completed. To the best of my knowledge, Professor Abrams is the first to suggest that there are radical differences between the "symbolist" and "romantic" theories of poetry.

[4] A brief summary of "Transcendental Aesthetic." In the *Critique of Pure Reason* imagination is just a bridge between perception and thought.

[5] "Schema" means in Kant a procedure by which the categories of the understanding are applied to the manifold of sensuous intuition.

[6] Samuel Taylor Coleridge, *Biographia Literaria*, ed. with introduction by George Watson (London, 1962), p. 49.

[7] *Ibid.*, p. 68.   [8] *Ibid.*, p. 79.   [9] *Ibid.*, p. 85.   [10] *Ibid.*, p. 86.

[11] Wellek, *A History of Modern Criticism, 1750–1950: The Romantic Age*, p. 74.

[12] My discussion of Coleridge below is centered on his ten theses and their implications (*Biographia*, pp. 149–155).

[13] *Philosophies of Art and Beauty: Selected Readings in Aesthetics from Plato to Heidegger*, ed. Albert Hofstadter and Richard Kuhns (New York, 1964), p. 354.

[14] *Ibid.*, p. 364.   [15] *Ibid.*, pp. 356, 362, 373.

[16] *Biographia*, p. 153.   [17] *Ibid.*, p. 155.

[18] *Ibid.*, p. 139.   [19] *Ibid.*, p. 152.   [20] *Ibid.*, p. 167.

[21] See Krieger, *The New Apologists*.

[22] See Krieger's *A Window to Criticism: Shakespeare's "Sonnets" and Modern Poetics* (Princeton, 1964).

[23] Wellek, first on Kant and then on Schelling: "Kant did most resolutely isolate the aesthetic realm from the realms of science, morality, and utility by arguing that the aesthetic state of mind differs profoundly from our perception of the pleasurable, the useful, the true, and the good. Kant invented the famous definition: aesthetic pleasure is 'disinterested satisfaction'" (*A History of Modern Criticism, 1750–1950: The Later Eighteenth Century* [New Haven, 1955], p. 229). "When in 1796, F. W. J. Schelling . . . drew up his program of a new philosophy, he completely ignored Kant's distinction between epistemology, ethics, and aesthetics. He put forward the grandiose claim that the idea of beauty, taken in the higher Platonic sense, 'unites all other ideas.' 'I am convinced,' he says, 'that the highest act of reason is the aesthetic act embracing all ideas and that truth and goodness are made kindred only in beauty.' While Kant was at great pains to distinguish between the good, the true, and the beautiful, Schelling enthrones beauty as the highest value. But his beauty is actually truth and goodness in disguise" (*The Romantic Age*, p. 74). See p. 3n, above.

[24] Abrams, *The Mirror and the Lamp*, p. 103.

[25] *Selections from Ralph Waldo Emerson*, ed. Stephen E. Whicher (Boston, 1960), p. 224.

[26] *Biographia*, p. 254.   [27] *Ibid.*, p. 172.   [28] *Ibid.*, p. 167.

[29] *Philosophies of Art and Beauty*, pp. 360, 362.

[30] *Biographia Literaria*, by S. T. Coleridge, edited with his Aes-

thetical Essays by J. Shawcross, II (London, 1907), 257 ("On Poesy or Art").

31 *Ibid.*, p. 243.

32 "The Splendors and Miseries of Courtesans," in *The Edition Definitive of the Comédie Humaine by Honoré de Balzac*, I (Philadelphia, 1895), x (Balzac's preface).

33 William Blake, *Poetry and Prose*, ed. Geoffrey Keynes (London, 1948), p. 869.

34 Wimsatt and Brooks, *Literary Criticism*, p. 424.

35 Technically speaking, it is impossible to do this, even in the context of idealistic philosophy. I am not, however, arguing Blake's inadequacy as a thinker, but merely trying to present his views.

36 Richard Hofstadter, *Social Darwinism in American Thought* (first published in 1944; Boston, 1960), p. 21.

37 Jacques Barzun, *Darwin, Marx, and Wagner* (first published 1941; Garden City, 1958), p. 67.

38 I found the following works especially helpful: Barzun, *Darwin, Marx, and Wagner;* C. C. Walcutt, *American Literary Naturalism: A Divided Stream* (Minneapolis, 1956); Stanley Edgar Hyman, *The Tangled Bank: Darwin, Marx, Frazer, and Freud as Imaginative Writers* (New York, 1962).

39 Barzun, *Darwin, Marx, and Wagner*, pp. 4, 7.

40 By "more sophisticated formulations" I refer specifically to contemporary logical positivists. See, for example, A. J. Ayer, *Language, Truth, and Logic* (first published 1935; New York, 1946), a book that incorporates much of the thinking of Carnap and Wittgenstein.

41 Wallace Stevens, *Opus Posthumous*, ed. with introduction by Samuel French Morse (London, 1959), p. 246.

42 Émile Zola, *The Experimental Novel, and Other Essays*, trans. Belle M. Sherman (New York, 1893), p. 1.

43 *Ibid.*, p. 2.   44 *Ibid.*, p. 7.   45 *Ibid.*, p. 18.

46 *Ibid.*, p. 23.   47 *Ibid.*, pp. 35, 44.   48 *Ibid.*, pp. 25–26.

49 T. E. Hulme, *Speculations*, ed. Herbert Read, with foreword by Jacob Epstein (New York, 1924), p. 3.

50 *Ibid.*, p. 5.

51 I am thinking especially of Hulme's essay on discontinuity, "Humanism and the Religious Attitude," and his two essays, "Bergson's Theory of Art" and "The Philosophy of Intensive Manifolds," which together suggest a contextual view of poetry.

52 *Kant: Selections*, ed. Theodore M. Greene (New York, 1929), p. 426.

53 This is the chief interpretation of symbolism. See John Senior, *The Way Down and Out: The Occult in Symbolist Literature* (Ithaca, 1959), and William York Tindall, *The Literary Symbol* (Bloomington, 1955), chap. 2, both of whom emphasize Swedenborgian "correspondence" in Blake and Baudelaire.

54 *Selected Writings of Edgar Allan Poe*, ed. E. H. Davidson (Boston, 1956), p. 414.

55 Allen Tate, "The Angelic Imagination: Poe as God," in *Collected Essays* (Denver, 1959), pp. 432–454.

56 *Poe*, p. 470.   57 *Ibid.*, p. 437.   58 *Ibid.*, p. 35.

[59] *Ibid.*, pp. 410, 411.   [60] *Ibid.*, p. 414.   [61] *Ibid.*, p. 412.
[62] *Ibid.*, p. 411.   [63] *Ibid.*, pp. 439, 470–471.   [64] *Ibid.*, p. 437.
[65] *Ibid.*, pp. 436–437, 470.   [66] *Ibid.*, p. 468.
[67] *Baudelaire on Poe: Critical Papers*, trans. and ed. Lois Hyslop
and Francis E. Hyslop, Jr. (Carrolltown, 1952), p. 85.
[68] See A. G. Lehmann, *The Symbolist Aesthetic in France, 1885–
1895* (Oxford, 1950), pp. 1–36.
[69] *Baudelaire on Poe*, p. 53.
[70] *Ibid.*, esp. the essay "New Notes on Edgar Poe."
[71] *Ibid.*, p. 139.   [72] *Ibid.*, p. 66.   [73] *Ibid.*, p. 137.
[74] Charles Feidelson, Jr., *Symbolism and American Literature* (first
published 1953; Chicago, 1965), p. 45.
[75] *The Mirror of Art: Critical Studies by Charles Baudelaire*, trans.
and ed. Jonathan Mayne (New York, 1955), pp. 232, 236, 238.
[76] *Mallarmé: Selected Prose Poems, Essays, and Letters*, trans. with
introduction by Bradford Cook (Baltimore, 1956), p. 15.
[77] *Ibid.*, p. 18.   [78] *Ibid.*, p. 22.   [79] *Ibid.*, p. 24.   [80] *Ibid.*, p. 30.
[81] *Ibid.*   [82] *Ibid.*, p. 10.   [83] *Ibid.*, p. 47.
[84] *Ibid.*, pp. 39–40. This argument also seems to anticipate William
K. Wimsatt, Jr.: ". . . behind a metaphor lies a resemblance between
two classes, and hence a more general third class. This class is unnamed and most likely remains unnamed and is apprehended only
through the metaphor" (*The Verbal Icon* [first published 1954; New
York, 1960], p. 79).
[85] *Mallarmé*, p. 38.
[86] *Ibid.*, pp. 40–41, 43, 81–82, 101.   [87] *Ibid.*, p. 41.
[88] *Ibid.*, p. 43. In connection with the incantatory elements in Mallarmé's aesthetic see Wallace Fowlie's comments in *Mallarmé* (Chicago, 1953), chap. 9, "The Poet as Ritualist." Of course, Fowlie recog-
nizes what I have called the contextual side of symbolist aesthetic:
". . . the meaning of a poetic work is inseparable from its structure"
(p. 233).
[89] Paul Valéry, *Variety: Second Series*, trans. W. A. Bradley (New
York, 1938), pp. 77, 92.
[90] *Ibid.*, p. 92.
[91] Paul Valéry, *The Art of Poetry*, trans. Denise Folliot, with
introduction by T. S. Eliot (New York, 1958), pp. 170–171, 180, 192.
[92] *Ibid.*, p. 177.   [93] *Ibid.*, p. 189.   [94] *Ibid.*, p. 178.
[95] *Ibid.*, p. 180.   [96] *Ibid.*, p. 183.

CHAPTER 3.

[1] *The Autobiography of William Butler Yeats* (New York, 1953),
p. 36 (hereinafter cited as *A*).
[2] *A*, esp. pp. 101–103.
[3] Richard Ellmann (*The Identity of Yeats* [New York, 1954], p. 1)
holds a similar position: "His themes and symbols are fixed in
youth, and then renewed with increasing vigor and directness to the
end of his life. . . . the more one reads Yeats, the more his works
appear to rotate in a few orbits."

⁴ A book very much concerned with the theoretical issues that I raise in this section is Jacques Maritain and Raissa Maritain, *The Situation of Poetry: Four Essays on the Relations of Poetry, Mysticism, Magic, and Knowledge* (New York, 1955).

⁵ *The Letters of W. B. Yeats*, ed. Allan Wade (New York, 1955), p. 403 (hereinafter cited as *Letters of WBY*).

⁶ *A*, p. 15.

⁷ *A*, pp. 50, 70–71, 74, 90–91, 96, 106, 160, 167, 214, 245, 263, 265.

⁸ W. B. Yeats, *Essays and Introductions* (New York, 1961), p. 28 (hereinafter cited as *E*).

⁹ *E*, p. 36.   ¹⁰ *E*, p. 52.   ¹¹ *Letters of WBY*, p. 63.

¹² *Ibid.*, p. 59.   ¹³ *Ibid.*, pp. 96–97.

¹⁴ Hazard Adams, "Some Yeatsean Versions of Comedy," in *In Excited Reverie: A Centenary Tribute to William Butler Yeats*, ed. A. Norman Jeffares and K. G. W. Cross (London, 1965), p. 152.

¹⁵ Jacques Barzun, *Darwin, Marx, and Wagner* (first published 1941; Garden City, 1958), pp. 105–106.

¹⁶ *A*, p. 54.   ¹⁷ *A*, p. 55.   ¹⁸ *Ibid.*   ¹⁹ *A*, p. 56.   ²⁰ *A*, p. 109.

²¹ *A*, p. 106.   ²² *A*, p. 110.   ²³ *A*, p. 111   ²⁴ *A*, p. 115

²⁵ *A*, p. 149.   ²⁶ *A*, p. 96.   ²⁷ *E*, p. 146.   ²⁸ *Ibid.*   ²⁹ *E*, p. 148.

³⁰ *E*, p. 150.   ³¹ *E*, p. 149.   ³² *E*, p. 155.   ³³ *E*, p. 157.

³⁴ *E*, p. 159.   ³⁵ *E*, p. 160.

³⁶ Eliseo Vivas, *The Artistic Transaction: Essays on the Theory of Literature* (Columbus, 1963). See the title essay.

³⁷ *E*, p. 163.   ³⁸ *E*, p. 159.   ³⁹ *E*, p. 163.   ⁴⁰ *E*, p. 189.

⁴¹ *E*, p. 190.   ⁴² *E*, pp. 191–192.   ⁴³ *E*, pp. 192–193.

⁴⁴ *E*, p. 193.

⁴⁵ On symbolist theory, see "The Theatre," "The Moods," and "Emotion of Multitude," in *E*, pp. 165–172, 195, 215–216. Yeats's friend, Arthur Symons, articulated similar magical views in *The Symbolist Movement in Literature*.

⁴⁶ See Hazard Adams, *Blake and Yeats: The Contrary Vision* (Ithaca, 1955), for the fullest account of Yeats's affiliations with romantic thought.

⁴⁷ *E*, p. 61.   ⁴⁸ *E*, p. 79.   ⁴⁹ *E*, p. 87.   ⁵⁰ *E*, p. 94.   ⁵¹ *E*, p. 112.

⁵² *E*, pp. 119–120.   ⁵³ *E*, pp. 128–129.   ⁵⁴ *E*, p. 145.

⁵⁵ Thomas Parkinson, "Yeats and Pound: The Illusion of Influence," *Comparative Literature*, VI (Summer, 1954), 264.

⁵⁶ *E*, p. 201.   ⁵⁷ *E*, p. 202.   ⁵⁸ *Letters of WBY*, p. 402.

⁵⁹ *Ibid.*, p. 403.   ⁶⁰ *A*, p. 116.

⁶¹ Yeats's philosophical naïveté emerges in *W. B. Yeats and T. Sturge Moore: Their Correspondence, 1901–1937*, ed. Ursula Bridge (New York, 1953), pp. 67–69, 80, 82, 85–87, 95–99.

⁶² *A*, p. 45.

⁶³ *A*, pp. 105, 150, 201, 279.

⁶⁴ *A*, p. 200.

⁶⁵ An extreme statement of the idea is I. A. Richards, *Science and Poetry* (London, 1935), p. 43: "As a rule the poet is not conscious of the reasons why just these words and no others serve best. They fall into their place without his conscious control. . . ."

66 W. B. Yeats, *Explorations* (New York, 1962), pp. 86–87 (hereinafter cited as *Ex*).

67 *Ex*, pp. 87–88. 68 *Ex*, p. 115. 69 *Ex*, p. 148. 70 *Ex*, p. 149.

71 *Ex*, p. 155. 72 *Ex*, pp. 194–195. 73 *Ex*, p. 196. 74 *Ibid*.

75 *Ex*, p. 200. 76 *Letters of WBY*, pp. 434–435. 77 *E*, p. 298.

78 *E*, p. 349. 79 *E*, p. 296. 80 *E*, p. 297. 81 *E*, p. 287.

82 *E*, p. 288. 83 *E*, p. 301; also p. 279. 84 *E*, p. 266.

85 *E*, p. 268. 86 *E*, pp. 271–272. 87 *E*, p. 251. 88 *E*, p. 252.

89 *E*, p. 253. 90 *E*, p. 254. 91 *E*, p. 255. 92 *E*, p. 253.

93 *E*, p. 229. 94 *E*, p. 243. 95 *Letters of WBY*, p. 608.

96 *E*, pp. 221, 224. 97 *E*, pp. 224, 226, 230. 98 *E*, p. 230.

99 *A*, pp. 279, 280–281, 285. 100 *A*, p. 306.

101 W. B. Yeats, *Mythologies* (New York, 1959), p. 344 (hereinafter cited as *M*).

102 *M*, pp. 356–357. 103 *M*, p. 358. 104 *M*, p. 364.

105 *M*, p. 366.

106 Quoted in A. Norman Jeffares, *W. B. Yeats: Man and Poet* (London, 1949), p. 351 (Appendix: "Genealogical Tree of Evolution").

107 *M*, p. 341.

108 W. B. Yeats, *A Vision* (New York, 1961), p. 40 (hereinafter cited as *V*).

109 *V*, pp. 71, 79, 94, 144, 187, 214, 236.

110 *V*, p. 194.

111 *V*, p. 219. In a footnote on the same page Yeats wrote: "Professor Bradley believed also that he could stand by the death-bed of wife or mistress and not long for an immortality of body and soul. He found it difficult to reconcile personal immortality with his form of Absolute idealism, and besides he hated the common heart; an arrogant, sapless man."

112 *Ex*, p. 309. 113 *Ex*, p. 336. 114 *E*, p. 405. 115 *E*, p. 448.

116 *E*, pp. 439, 445. 117 *E*, p. 509. 118 *E*, p. 522.

119 *Letters of WBY*, p. 55. For a comment on "Dhoya" which is similar to my own see Alex Zwerdling, "W. B. Yeats: Variations on the Visionary Quest," *University of Toronto Quarterly*, XXX (Oct., 1960), 72–85.

120 *The Collected Works of William Butler Yeats*, VII (Stratford-on-Avon, 1908), 292.

121 *Ibid*. 122 *Ibid*., p. 293. 123 *M*, pp. 68–69. 124 *M*, p. 77.

125 *M*, pp. 28–29.

126 The stories that contain elements of double vision are "The Golden Age," "Mortal Help," "Dust Hath Closed Helen's Eye," "A Voice," "Kidnappers," and "The Three O'Byrnes and the Evil Faeries."

127 An interesting footnote to this problem, and to the problem of belief, is "Stories of Michael Robartes and His Friends: An Extract from a Record Made by His Pupils," *A Vision*, pp. 33–55. Along with the comical main story of how the "system" was discovered, there are two parallel stories of artists who, lacking practical sense and worldly understanding, are sexual buffoons and incompetents. Living totally in the head, they fail below the waist.

128 *M*, p. 267. 129 *M*, p. 269. 130 *M*, p. 273.

[131] *M*, pp. 276, 277, 280. [132] *M*, p. 289. [133] *M*, pp. 278–279.
[134] *M*, pp. 286–287.

CHAPTER 4.

[1] John Unterecker, *A Reader's Guide to William Butler Yeats* (New York, 1962), p. 168.
[2] F. A. C. Wilson, *W. B. Yeats and Tradition* (London, 1958), p. 15.
[3] *The Letters of W. B. Yeats*, ed. Allan Wade (New York, 1955), p. 63 (hereinafter cited as *Letters of WBY*).
[4] *The Collected Poems of W. B. Yeats* (New York, 1963), p. 355 (hereinafter cited as *CP*).
[5] *CP*, pp. 357, 359. [6] *CP*, p. 356. [7] *CP*, p. 361. [8] *CP*, p. 379.
[9] *CP*, p. 351. [10] *CP*, p. 18. [11] *CP*, p. 19. [12] *CP*, pp. 7–8.
[13] *CP*, p. 9. [14] "The Madness of King Goll," *CP*, pp. 16–18.
[15] *CP*, p. 49. [16] See *Letters of WBY*, pp. 99–100. [17] *CP*, p. 40.
[18] *CP*, p. 41. [19] *CP*, pp. 47–48. [20] *CP*, p. 32. [21] *Ibid.* [22] *Ibid.*
[23] *CP*, p. 33. [24] *CP*, p. 31. [25] *CP*, p. 54. [26] *CP*, p. 56.
[27] See "The Wind among the Reeds," "The Everlasting Voices," "The Moods," "The Unappeasable Host," "The Song of Wandering Aengus," "The Heart of the Woman," "He Mourns for the Change . . . ," "He Bids His Beloved Be at Peace," "He Remembers Forgotten Beauty," "The Valley of the Black Pig," "The Lover Asks Forgiveness for His Many Moods," "He Hears the Cry of the Sedge," "The Secret Rose."
[28] *Letters of WBY*, p. 84.
[29] Thomas Parkinson, *W. B. Yeats, Self-Critic: A Study of His Early Verse* (Berkeley and Los Angeles, 1951), and *W. B. Yeats: The Later Poetry* (Berkeley and Los Angeles, 1964).
[30] *CP*, p. 78. [31] *CP*, p. 124.
[32] Two articles I found particularly suggestive are William Empson, "Mr. Wilson on the Byzantium Poems," *Review of English Literature*, I (July, 1960), 51–56; G. S. Fraser, "Yeats's Byzantium," *Critical Quarterly*, II (Autumn, 1960), 253–261. The possibility of an "ironist" reading of the Byzantium poems was suggested first by Cleanth Brooks in an essay which (curiously) is thoroughly doctrinal, leaning on the Yeatsian system for its central claims (see *Modern Poetry and the Tradition* [Chapel Hill, 1939], pp. 173–202).
[33] W. K. Wimsatt's brief aside in *Hateful Contraries* (Lexington, 1965), p. 23, deserves to be quoted: "Probably no man has kept up, eked out, teased along so successfully, through closing phases of a long career, the sense of uncertainty and noncommittal, of ironic unrest. . . . Yeats I think may be said to have attained to something like a maximum technical knowledge of how the cultivation of the contraries is maintained."
[34] W. B. Yeats, *A Vision* (New York, 1961), p. 279.
[35] Wilhelm Worringer, *Abstraction and Empathy*, trans. Michael Bullock (New York, 1953).

36 On this point see Parkinson, *W. B. Yeats: The Later Poetry.*
37 *A Vision*, pp. 144, 219.
38 A good deal of light is cast on the second Byzantium poem by the earlier drafts, reprinted in Curtis Bradford, "Yeats's Byzantium Poems: A Study of Their Development," *PMLA*, LXXV (March, 1960), 110–125.
39 *W. B. Yeats and Tradition*, p. 236.

CHAPTER 5.

1 Wallace Stevens, *Opus Posthumous*, ed. with introduction by Samuel French Morse (London, 1959), p. 244 (hereinafter cited as *OP*).
2 *OP*, p. 246.   3 *OP*, p. 244.
4 See Frank Doggett, "Wallace Stevens' River That Flows Nowhere," *Chicago Review*, XV (Summer–Autumn, 1962), 67–80.
5 *OP*, pp. 206–207.
6 Wallace Stevens, *The Necessary Angel: Essays on Reality and the Imagination* (London, 1955), p. 21 (hereinafter cited as *NA*).
7 *NA*, p. 22.   8 *NA*, pp. 118–119.
9 Ernst Cassirer, *Language and Myth*, trans. Susanne K. Langer (New York, 1946), p. 7.
10 *OP*, pp. 163, 166.   11 *NA*, p. 56.   12 *OP*, p. 241.
13 *NA*, p. 136.
14 Ernst Cassirer, *An Essay on Man* (first published 1944; New Haven, 1962), pp. 155–156.
15 *Ibid.*, p. 156.   16 *NA*, pp. 137–38.   17 *NA*, p. 138.
18 *OP*, p. 210.   19 *OP*, p. 161.   20 *OP*, p. 261.
21 See *OP*, p. 213; *NA*, pp. 6, 22, 85.
22 *NA*, p. 7.
23 Wallace Stevens, *Collected Poems* (London, 1955), p. 424.
24 See *OP*, p. 220: "One of the motives in writing is renewal."
25 *OP*, p. 213.   26 *NA*, p. 54.   27 *OP*, p. 160.
28 Quoted in Jacques Barzun, *Darwin, Marx, and Wagner* (first published 1941; Garden City, 1958), p. 67.
29 See, for example, *OP*, p. 166 and *NA*, p. 10.
30 *OP*, p. 218.
31 *OP*, p. 219; see also *OP*, pp. 226–229 *passim*.
32 *NA*, pp. 20, 60.   33 *NA*, pp. 13–14.   34 *NA*, pp. 14, 16.
35 *OP*, p. 174.
36 *Kant: Selections*, ed. Theodore M. Greene (New York, 1929), p. 426.
37 Cassirer, *Language and Myth*, p. 8.   38 *Ibid.*, p. 11.
39 *NA*, p. 74.   40 *NA*, pp. 13–14.   41 *NA*, p. 17.   42 *NA*, p. 32.
43 *OP*, p. 217.   44 *OP*, p. 206.   45 *OP*, pp. 196–197.
46 *NA*, p. 62.
47 See, typically, *NA*, pp. 22–23, 26–27, 30–31.
48 *NA*, p. 150.   49 *NA*, p. 65.   50 *OP*, p. 159.   51 *NA*, p. 141.
52 *NA*, p. 171.   53 *NA*, p. 165.   54 *OP*, pp. 216–229.

[55] *OP*, p. 173. [56] *NA*, pp. 31, 173; *OP*, p. 163.

[57] William York Tindall has also noticed this duality; see his *Wallace Stevens* (Minneapolis, 1961), p. 31.

[58] *NA*, p. 57. [59] *NA*, p. 27. [60] *OP*, p. 165. [61] *OP*, p. 225.

[62] *OP*, p. 157.

[63] For the feeling of "abstraction" see *NA*, pp. 23, 139; *OP*, p. 169.

[64] Paul Valéry, "Dialogues," trans. William McCaucland Stewart, with two prefaces by Wallace Stevens (New York, 1956), p. 126. This is the fourth volume in *The Collected Works of Paul Valéry*, ed. Jackson Mathews.

[65] *Ibid.*, p. 127. [66] *Ibid.*, p. 121. [67] *Ibid.*, p. 123.

[68] *Ibid.*, p. 131. [69] *NA*, p. 139.

[70] *NA*, pp. 30, 31. The poet is seen as "giving" savor to life on the one hand; on the other "he gives to life the supreme fictions."

[71] *NA*, pp. 30–31. [72] *NA*, p. 6. [73] *NA*, pp. 150–151.

[74] George Santayana, *The Life of Reason* (New York, 1954), p. 343.

[75] *OP*, p. 180. [76] *OP*, p. 163. [77] *NA*, p. 173. [78] *OP*, p. 213.

[79] *NA*, p. 63. [80] *NA*, p. 31. [81] *NA*, p. 76. [82] *NA*, p. 71.

[83] *NA*, p. 72. [84] *NA*, p. 73. [85] *OP*, p. 179. [86] *Ibid.*

[87] *NA*, p. 77. Note that metaphor operates by means of metamorphosis as defined in *NA*, p. 72.

[88] *NA*, p. 76. [89] *NA*, p. 75. [90] *NA*, p. 114.

[91] Philip Wheelwright, *Metaphor and Reality* (Bloomington, 1962), p. 51.

[92] *Ibid.*, p. 85. [93] *NA*, p. 79. [94] *NA*, p. 80. [95] *NA*, p. 14.

[96] Sigmund Freud, "The Future of an Illusion," in *The Standard Edition of the Complete Psychological Works of Sigmund Freud*, ed. and trans. James Strachey, XXI (London, 1961), 56.

[97] *Ibid.*, p. 75. [98] *Ibid.*, p. 80. [99] *NA*, p. 51.

CHAPTER 6.

[1] *The Act of the Mind: Essays on the Poetry of Wallace Stevens*, ed. J. Hillis Miller and Roy Harvey Pearce (Baltimore, 1965), p. ix. The editors conclude with the proselytizing fervor that is characteristic of so much Stevens criticism: "Reading the poems, studying the acts of the poet's mind, we may discover the ideas which could, or should, become ours." Similarly, Harold Bloom, but from the romantic point of view: "If we are to understand Wallace Stevens, if we are indeed to follow Stevens in the difficult task of rescuing him and ourselves from his and our own ironies, then we need to have these two ancestral poets [Emerson and Whitman] at their strongest" ("The Central Man: Emerson, Whitman, Wallace Stevens," *Massachusetts Review*, VII [Winter, 1966], 34). And Joseph Riddel, *The Clairvoyant Eye: The Poetry and Poetics of Wallace Stevens* (Baton Rouge, 1965), p. 230: ". . . he had finally satisfied himself that 'God and the imagination are one.'" I agree with Louis Martz's assumption: "His later poems re-explore and re-state, but do not centrally modify

[his] view of the imagination's role in life" (*The Poem of the Mind: Essays on Poetry, English and American* [New York, 1966], p. 184). And it is my point that Stevens' view is consistently ironic.

2 Wallace Stevens, *Opus Posthumous,* ed. with introduction by Samuel French Morse (London, 1959), p. 195 (hereinafter cited as *OP*).

3 *OP*, p. 192.

4 R. P. Blackmur, *Form and Value in Modern Poetry* (Garden City, 1957), p. 222.

5 See "The Irrational Element in Poetry," *OP*, p. 221.

6 Randall Jarrell, *Poetry and the Age* (New York, 1962), p. 131.

7 Kenneth Burke, *Counter-Statement* (first published 1931; Chicago, 1957), p. 102.

8 Wallace Stevens, *Collected Poems* (London, 1955), p. 247 (hereinafter cited as *CP*).

9 *CP*, p. 485.   10 *OP*, p. 167.

11 Wallace Stevens, *The Necessary Angel: Essays on Reality and the Imagination* (London, 1955), p. 56 (hereinafter cited as *NA*).

12 *CP*, p. 67.   13 *CP*, p. 165.   14 *CP*, p. 425.   15 *CP*, p. 70.

16 *CP*, p. 58.   17 *CP*, p. 522.   18 *CP*, pp. 355-356.   19 *CP*, p. 305.

20 *CP*, pp. 9–10.   21 *CP*, p. 468.

22 Blackmur, *Form and Value,* p. 198.

23 A. G. Lehmann, *The Symbolist Aesthetic in France, 1885–1895* (Oxford, 1950), esp. pp. 1–35.

24 *CP*, p. 104.   25 *CP*, p. 14.

26 *CP*, p. 246. I am deeply indebted to Eugene Nassar, *Wallace Stevens: An Anatomy of Figuration* (Philadelphia, 1965), an indispensable guide to Stevens' figures.

27 In another section of "Le Monocle" (*CP*, p. 15) Stevens writes:

When amorists grow bald, then amours shrink
Into the compass and curriculum
Of introspective exiles, lecturing.
It is a theme for Hyacinth alone.

28 *CP*, p. 328.   29 *CP*, p. 222.   30 *CP*, p. 10.   31 *CP*, p. 12.

32 *CP*, p. 471.   33 See, especially, *CP*, pp. 144, 185.

34 *CP*, p. 119.   35 *CP*, pp. 471–472.

36 Blackmur, *Form and Value,* p. 222.

37 *CP*, p. 380.   38 *CP*, p. 363.   39 *Ibid.*   40 *CP*, p. 381.   41 *Ibid.*

42 In "Add This to Rhetoric" (*CP*, p. 198) Stevens writes (italics mine):

. . . In the way you speak
You arrange, the thing is posed,
What in nature merely grows

Tomorrow when the sun,
For all your images,
Comes up as the sun, *bull fire,*
Your images will have left
No shadow of themselves.

43 *CP*, p. 129.

44 In "Local Objects" (*OP*, pp. 111–112) Stevens speaks of

The few things, the objects of insight, the integrations
Of feeling, the things that come of their own accord,
Because he desired without quite knowing what,

That were the moments of the classic, the beautiful.
I find it interesting that of all his "ideas of order," Stevens appears to accept as legitimate and honest only those that are not ideas, strictly speaking, but moments of feeling.

[45] Harold Bloom, "Notes toward a Supreme Fiction: A Commentary," in Wallace Stevens: A Collection of Critical Essays, ed. Marie Borroff (Englewood Cliffs, 1963), pp. 76–95.

[46] CP, pp. 403–404.   [47] CP, p. 404.   [48] CP, p. 406.

[49] Riddel, The Clairvoyant Eye, p. 230, has ignored the qualification "We say" in "Final Soliloquy of the Interior Paramour."

[50] CP, pp. 96–97.   [51] CP, pp. 97–98.   [52] CP, p. 155.

[53] CP, p. 239.   [54] CP, p. 240.

[55] Joseph Riddel, " 'Poets' Politics'—Wallace Stevens' Owl's Clover," Modern Philology, LVI (Nov., 1958), 120–121.

[56] CP, p. 240.

[57] See the discussion above in this chapter.

[58] Yvor Winters, On Modern Poets (New York, 1959), p. 23.

[59] CP, p. 19.   [60] See discussion above in chapter 5.   [61] CP, p. 19.

[62] CP, p. 198.   [63] CP, p. 332.   [64] CP, p. 288.   [65] CP, p. 128.

[66] See Frank Kermode, Wallace Stevens (London, 1960), pp. 37, 57–58; and Marius Bewley, "Romanticism Reconsidered," Hudson Review, XVII (Spring, 1964), 127. Surprisingly, "Key West" has rarely been closely analyzed by Stevens' critics. Most recently Joseph Riddel, in The Clairvoyant Eye, pp. 117–120, makes romantic claims for Stevens, seeing in the poem a "marriage of subject and object."

[67] René Wellek persuasively argues that underlying romantic poetics is the theory that subject and object, self and nature, spiritually cohere and fuse. See, for example, his two essays on romanticism in Concepts of Criticism, ed. and with introduction by Steven G. Nichols (New Haven, 1963).

[68] CP, p. 122.

[69] Jacques Maritain, Creative Intuition in Art and Poetry (New York, 1953), p. 43.

[70] Arthur Mizener, "Not in Cold Blood," Kenyon Review, XII (Spring, 1951), 222–223.

[71] CP, p. 326.

[72] See, for example, OP, pp. 160, 161, 163: "The real is only the base. But it is the base"; "In poetry at least the imagination must not detach itself from reality"; "All our ideas come from the natural world."

[73] See CP, pp. 97–98, 471, 473.

[74] NA, p. 75: "One may find intimations of immortality in an object on the mantelpiece; and these intimations are as real in the mind in which they occur as the mantelpiece itself. Even if they are only a part of an adult make-believe, the whole point is that the structure of reality because of the range of resemblances that it contains is measurably an adult make-believe."

Index

"Letter to B——" (Poe), 30, 31

Literary theory: questions asked by, 4-5

Locke, John, 41, 66; epistemology of, contrasted with Kant's, 10; and naturalist theory, 21, 24

Mallarmé, Stéphane, 29, 31, 80, 135, 138, 150, 169; and Poe, 35; on romantic idealism, 35; on naturalistic theory, 35; on imagination, 35-36; contextualism, 35-37; and Wheelwright, 36; symbolist theory of language, 36; and impersonality, 64, 71

Maritain, Jacques, 180, 197 n. 4

Martz, Louis, 202 n. 1

Marx, Karl, 23, 24, 41, 64, 122, 176

Mathers, MacGregor, 41, 46; Yeats on, 48

Miller, J. Hillis, 193 n. 2; on Stevens, 201-202 n. 1

Mizener, Arthur, 181

Moore, T. Sturge, 80

Nassar, Eugene, vii, 178; as guide to Stevens' figures, 202 n. 26

Naturalistic theory: and transcendentalism, 3; defined, 20-21; compared with romantic theory, 21-22, 25-26, 122, 123-128; theory of reality in, 22-24; epistemology in, 22-24; and existentialism, 24-25; compared with symbolist theory, 28; as influence on Yeats, 43, 47-48, 55; as antipathetic to Yeats, 49, 51, 54-55; and poetics of will, 62-63; Yeats's denial of determinism in, 65, 72-74; determinism in, 86-87; as Stevens' orientation, 121-128, 133-134; Cassirer on, 123-124; Stevens' escape

from determinism of, 128-131; summarized, 188

New Romantics, The (Foster), 9

"Northrop Frye and Contemporary Criticism: Ariel and the Spirit of Gravity" (Krieger), 30 n

"On Poesy or Art" (Coleridge), 18-20

"On the Principles of Genial Criticism" (Coleridge), 3 n

"On the Relation of the Plastic Arts to Nature" (Schelling): influence of, on Coleridge, 19

Organicism: Coleridge's theory of, vs. contextual theory, 17-20

Parkinson, Thomas, 98; on Yeats-Pound relationship, 59-60

Pearce, Roy Harvey: on Stevens, 201-202 n. 1

"Philosophy of Composition, The" (Poe), 34

Play and Place of Criticism, The (Krieger), 6 n, 30 n

Poe, Edgar Allan, 27, 29, 31, 37, 38; as magical symbolist, 30; as antiromantic, 31-32; as contextualist, 34; as affectivist, 34 n

Poetics of will: defined in Yeats and Stevens, 6-7; as antiwill (or imagination) in Kantian tradition, 6 n; and Murray Krieger's notions in "The Existential Basis of Contextualist Criticism," 6-7 n; defined in Yeats, 58-59, 60, 62-74; naturalistic backgrounds in Yeats, 62-63, 68, 69; as existentialist, 62-63, 192; and imaginative freedom in Yeats, 63-64, 72-74, 75-77, 80-81; and impersonality in Yeats, 64-68, 71-74; and imaginative freedom in Stevens, 129; defined in Ste-